# E-RESOURCES FOR TEACHING AND LEARNING

# E-RESOURCES FOR TEACHING AND LEARNING

*Edited by*

**Dr. S.K. Panneer Selvam**

*Assistant Professor*
*Department of Education*
*Bharathidasan University*
*Tiruchirappalli*
*Tamil Nadu*
*(India)*

DPH

**DISCOVERY PUBLISHING HOUSE PVT. LTD.**
**NEW DELHI-110 002**

*Published by:*
**Tilak Wasan**
**DISCOVERY PUBLISHING HOUSE PVT. LTD.**
4383/4A, Ansari Road, Darya Ganj
New Delhi-110 002 (India)
*Phone* : +91-11-23279245, 43596064-65
*Fax* : +91-11-23253475
*E-mail* : parul.wasan@gmail.com
discoverypublishinghouse@gmail.com
*web* : www.discoverypublishinggroup.com

***First Edition:* 2012**

**ISBN: 978-93-5056-079-2**

**E-Resources for Teaching and Learning**



***Printed at:***
***Shree Balaji Art Press***
***Delhi***

# Preface

This is a compiled edition. The very purpose of this edition is to make the students and the teachers know what is going on around them in the academic world. Every small change taking place in human activities change the world in total. The world is changing by leaps and bounds during the present century. Innovating and evolving technologies revolutionize the existing IT scenario. We are able to come across venturing Tamils all over the world. I request to state that the upcoming generations of Tamil people living abroad do not recognize the importance of Tamil. They are not fond of it; World Wide Web will primarily be more effective in co-coordinating all the Tamils living all over the world. It will pave a way for orientation; we have to simplify the modern communication processes so that it is accessible even to the poorest of the poor.

Children of Tamil people living in foreign lands will be able to learn Tamil language, history of Tamil people, social and cultural traditions of glorious Tamil land, through Internet linking. Aeroplane and Telephone once thoroughly changed the life style of people across the world. In the same way computer technology have affected and changed all walks of life all over the world. The peerless influence of computer among the growing younger generation is tremendous. Human society as a whole is transformed into knowledge society by the lightening like quick functioning of computers in bringing out the skills lurking in the remote regions of brain. I acknowledge their whole hearted thanks again and again. This book provides an illuminations and in-depth analysis of modern technology's learning.

All the articles are taken from the INFITT website-who gave the eminent persons in the field of IT to UTHAMAM of world Tamil union. The very purpose of this edition is to make the students and the teachers know what is going on around them in the academic world. Even the entrepreneurs in the realm of education find it more beneficial. Some of the articles are modified or simplified versions. As the author I am not able to trace out and contact the resource persons who were helpful in bringing out this book. I acknowledge their whole hearted thanks again and again.

**Dr. S.K. Panneerselvam**

# Contents

# List of Contributors

1. P. Vasuki and C. Aravindan, SSN College of Engineering, Chennai, Tamil Nadu, India
2. Kasi Arumugam
3. Vijayalakshmi, S.R, Assistant Professor, School of IT and Science, Dr. GRD College of Science, Coimbatore-14
4. Syed Hussain
5. E. Iniya Nehru, Technical Director, National Informatics Centre, Tamil Nadu State Centre, Chennai
6. G. Amirtharaj, Software Engineer, Dr. A James, Consultant Dr. P. R. Nakkeeran Director, Tamil Virtual University, Taramani, Chennai - 600113,
7. V. Thangavel, SCSVMV University, Kancheepuram-631 561
8. V.Thangavel, SCSVMV University, Kancheepuram-631 561 Dr. V. Ramesh, Dept of Chemistry, Kalsar College of Engg. Mannur, Sriperumpudhur, Chennai- 602 105
9. A. Kovalan, Siva Pillai
10. Prof. B. Jagadhesan, D.B. Jain College (Autonomous), Chennai-97
11. Richards Hadlee, Computer Science, Loyola College, Chennai R. E. Iniya Nehru, Technical Director, NIC, Chennai
12. Dr. Mrs. A. Pethalakshmi, Mrs. R. Raja Rajeswari, M.V.M Government Arts College for Women,Dindigul
13. S. Srividhya, Student, M.C.A-CEG Anna University, Chennai-600 025

    Dr.T.Mala, Lecturer, Anna University Chennai-600 025.
14. Sobha Lalitha Devi, Pattabhi R K Rao T, Vijay Sundar Ram R, Au-KBC Research Centre, MIT campus of Anna University, Chennai-600 044

15. T V Geetha, Ranjani Parthasarathi and Madhan Karky, College of Engineering Guindy, Anna University
16. S. Swarnalatha, 24, K.G Gardens, Vartharajapuram, Coimbatore-641015
17. Abirami. S, Vilvanathan. K and Baskaran. R, CEG, Anna University, Chennai–25
18. P. Chellappan, Partner, Palaniappa Bros
19. Dr V. Krishnamoorthy (Former Professor of Anna University), 5, Srivatsa Apartments, A1-11, 23rd Cross Street, Besant Nagar, Chennai-600 090
20. A. Elangovan, MD-Cadgraf Digitals and Digiscape Gallery, Chennai
21. P. Arulmozhi, Project Associate, MILE Lab, Department of EE, IISc, Bangalore.
    A.G. Ramakrishnan, Professor, Department of EE, IISc, Bangalore.
22. Premalatha. R, SCSVMV University, Kanchipuram, Tamilnadu, India
    Srinivasan.S, Tamilnadu Open University, Chennai, Tamilnadu, India
23. Shashikiran K, MILE Lab, Dept of Electrical Engineering, Indian Institute of Science, Bangalore 560 012
    Swapnil Belhe, Gist Group, CDAC Pune
24. T. Jayasankar, Lecturer/ECE, Anna University Trichy
    Dr. J. Arputha Vijaya Selvi, Professor, Kings College of Engg,
    Prof. R. Rajendran, Tamil University, Pudukkottai Thanjavur
25. C. P. Santhosh Kumar, Amrita Vishwa Vidyapeetham, Coimbatore
    N. Deiva Sundaram, Madras University, Chennai

# 1

# Voice-based Tamizh Tutoring System for Primary School Children to Enhance Their Tamizh Learning Interest

— *P. Vasuki and C. Aravindan*

**ABSTRACT**

*In this chapter, we focus on interactive tamizh learning system for children. Our system displays a picture and asks the child to recognize the picture and to speak out its name. Our speech engine captures and analyses the speech to give proper feedback. The speech engine has been trained with a corpus of words to obtain probability distributions (templates) of spectral coefficients of words. Spectral coefficients of the input speech are extracted and the word is recognized by matching the spectral coefficients with the templates. This word is then compared to the original text of the picture being displayed. By making many trials at different levels, the system induces the child to utter the object identity in tamizh. A scoring system runs at the background to calculate scores based on number of fouls and success. Providing picture along with the word helps the child to easily register the word in written form and meaning of it. The child who receives such training will acquire quick tamizh reading and speaking capacity. The conceptual mapping of images with words improves the declarative knowledge of a child.*

***Keywords*** *— Speech Recognition, Computer-based Training, Tamizh Tutoring System, and Hidden Markov Model*

## INTRODUCTION

Pure class room teaching may be monotonous and computer based training acts as good supplement to it. Computer based training becomes more effective when it has a speech interface. Such systems are popular in foreign countries, but not available in tamizh, as there is less focus in tamizh speech processing. The system that we have designed provides a friendly environment for children and enables them to talk to the system in tamizh, while learning tamizh. Thus our system may help to motivate learning of tamizh and makes it joyful and interesting.

The Declarative knowledge is factual or experimental[7]. Displaying an object, pronouncing it, displaying its text and make a child to realize and later recognize improves declarative knowledge of the child and enables the child to map the word with real meaning of it. The child is active while learning by using her psychomotor skills, i.e. the child talks to the system using mike, uses keyboard and mouse for navigation and also using her cognitive skills to recognize the picture by looking it, recall, utter it correctly, learn to utter, learn to read.

The system gets speech input using omni directional mike and records the speech in wav format. The speech characteristics vary at each instant, each speaker even for same word. Thus we have gone for extensive training with ten speakers of various age groups and ten utterance of each word;

i.e. every word is trained with hundred instances of utterance. Likewise the system is trained with hundred and twenty five basic tamizh words which are collected from first standard tamizh book.

HTK toolkit (Hidden Markov Model Toolkit) is used for building the speech engine[6]. The speech samples are parameterized in the form of Mel Frequency Cepstral Coefficients (MFCC) which reflects the characteristics of perception. In training, the word is divided into 'n' states. For each state an acoustic model is generated based on Gaussian Mixture Model (GMM). The probability of each state initialized and re-estimated based on its sequence using Forward Backward algorithm. HMM Model is generated for each word as initial state probability and sequence of states with transition probability.

In testing, MFCC features of testing word are generated and mapped against the model of each and every word in the vocabulary set, using Viterbi Decoding Techniques. The training wave gets the label of the word that closely matches with highest score. If the word uttered is not the original name of picture, it plays a sound of it with the help of look up table. A scoring system is running at the back to calculate the score and when the child quits, the score is displayed.

## ARCHITECTURE

The project is of two phases (*i*) tamizh Speech engine (*ii*) Tamizh Tutoring system.

In first phase, Speech Engine has been developed with extended training with different speakers and various words. The speech Engine recognizes the word and converts into text. In second phase is tamizh tutoring system is implemented with speech interface on the top of speech engine. Fig. 1.1 shows the architecture of the complete system.

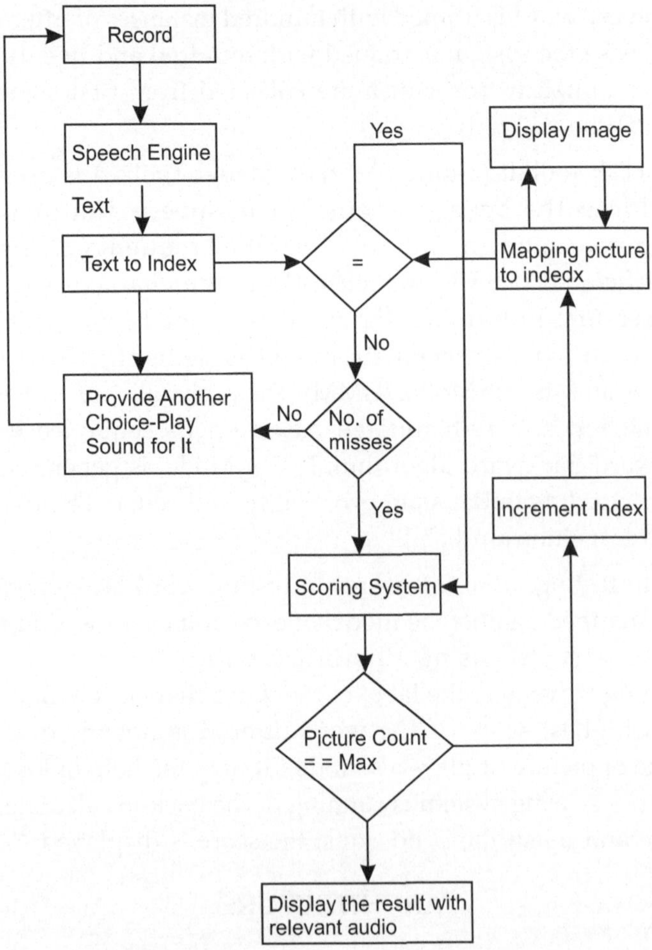


**Fig. 1.1 : Architecture of the Complete System**

## Speech Engine

Our Speech engine is an Isolated Speech Recognizer (ISR) implemented using Hidden Markov model. It takes isolated word as a processing unit recognize it and produces text. The system's word error rate is less when tested against system gets input as isolated word than connected word recognition.

Our tamizh tutoring system needs only isolated speech recognition.

## A. Data Preparation

### (i) Corpus Collection

The speech Corpus has been collected from 10 speakers of different ages( 6 year to 44 years) and different gender with sampling frequency of 16 khz and at 16 bit quantisation rate. They read 120 words in neutral form. Every speaker utters each word 10 times. The words are annotated manually. The signal is preprocessed before training.

Windowing is done to avoid the discontinuities of frames at stating and end[2]. The signal is divided into frames and windowed using hamming window of size 20 ms with the overlapping window size of 15 ms.

$$S_a^{'} = 0.54 - 0.46 \cos\left[2\pi(n-1)/N-1\right]S_2 \qquad ...(1)$$

### (ii) Feature Extraction

For each frame MFCC Mel frequency cepstral Coefficients are calculated. MFCC is a representation of the short-term power spectrum of a sound, based on linear cosine transform of a log power spectrum on a non-linear mel scale of frequency[4].

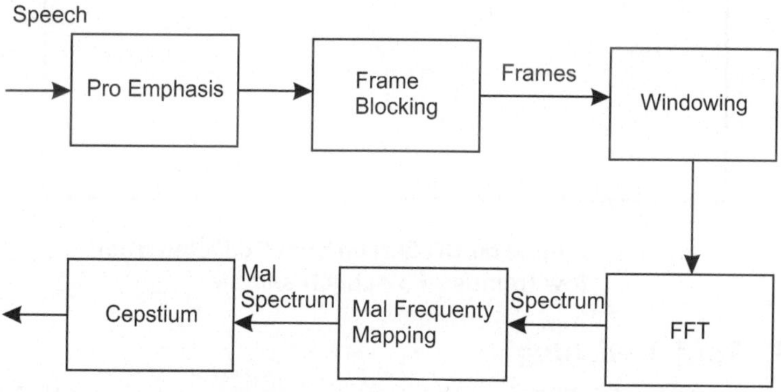


**Fig. 1.2 : Derivation of MFCC from Speech Samples.**

Fig. 1.2. shows the processing steps of deriving MFCC from speech.

MFCC -Mel frequency coefficients are working based on perception of word by human ear. Mel frequency Cepstral coefficients are 12 filters output that have been collected from the short time frame.

MFCC Feature vector of size 39 represents the signal of the frame. 13 parameter value (12 MFFCC coefficients and absolute energy of the frame), 13 delta coefficients (variation of cepstral coefficients between consecutive frames) and 13 acceleration coefficients are calculated for each frame. Fig. 1.3 shows the screen shot of MFCC collected from different frames of a speech sample.

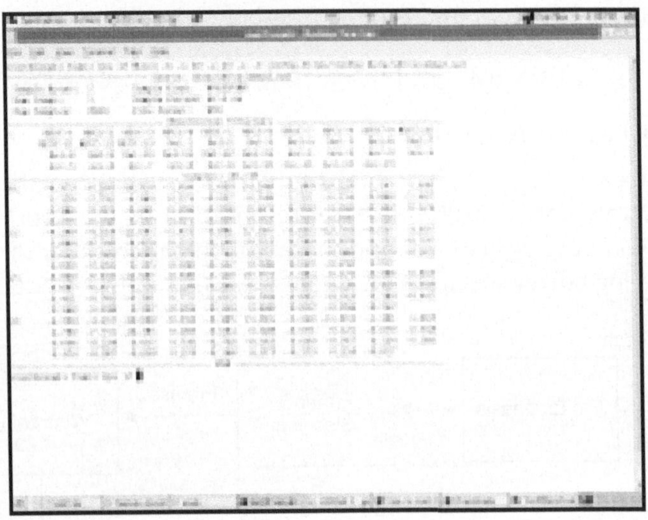

**Fig. 1.3 : Sample MFCC Screen Shot Collected from fow frames of a speech sample**

### *B. Word Modelling*

The quantized MFCC parameters are used to construct a HMM model for each word. HMM—Hidden Markov Model is as an efficient approach for short time stationary stochastic sequence[4]. Thus speech signal is modelled using Hidden Markov model[9].

In HMM training, HMM Model is created for each and every word in the training set. The Model is (A, B), where is the initial probability distribution, A is state transition probability and B is output probability. For a class whose data is considered to have multiple clusters, a Gaussian mixture model can be used to represent its probability distribution. The signal is represented by N (μ, σ). The output probability is estimated using Gaussian Parameter. The state transition probability is calculated based on state changes.

### C. HMM Parameter Initialization

The word should be divided into number of sequential states. Number of states is fixed for each word. We use three utterances of a word to form a mixture. HMM parameter template is created with initial values of mean 0.0 and variance is 1.0 for the 39 feature vectors. Gaussian Mixture model is used to find the probability distribution of the state of every mixture using expectation Maximisation algorithm. The signal is represented using Gaussian distribution using the formula[4]

$$N\left(\mu,\alpha^2\right)=\frac{1}{\sqrt{2\pi\sigma^2}} \tag{2}$$

### D. HMM Parameter Re Estimation

The word is divided equally into number of states based on timing. The frame is expected to belong to a certain state. With that expectation the mean and variance of every state is calculated. The probability of each frame belonging to the corresponding state specified is calculated based on the mean, variance of that state and feature value of that frame. If the probability maximize the frame belongingness in that specified state the frame is retained there else moved to the other state where its probability of belongingness is more. Thus the HRest tool used to re estimate HMM parameters using Baum Welch Algorithm. Baum Welch algorithm estimates the probability in the forward backward sequence. i.e. the probability of n'th frame is calculated from the previous n-1 frame, in Backward algorithm the probability of n'th frame is calculated from the remaining n+1 to N frames. HMM Parameters are defined based on forward and backward probabilities.An acoustic model has been generated for every word as a sequence of states.

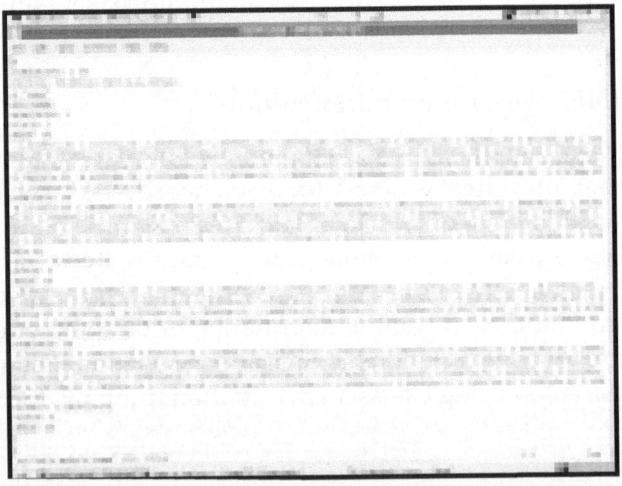

**Fig. 1.4 : Reestimated other HMM Parameter after applying forward backward algorithm**

### *E. Word Net (Language Model) formation*

Word net describes about the different sequence about the word occurrence and the probability of the sequence[5]. The apriori knowledge about the sequence of states improves the performance of speech recognition system[10]. Dictionary defines the grammar about the sequence of word occurrence. Our system recognize only isolated words, thus dictionary is formed such as individual word as single entity.

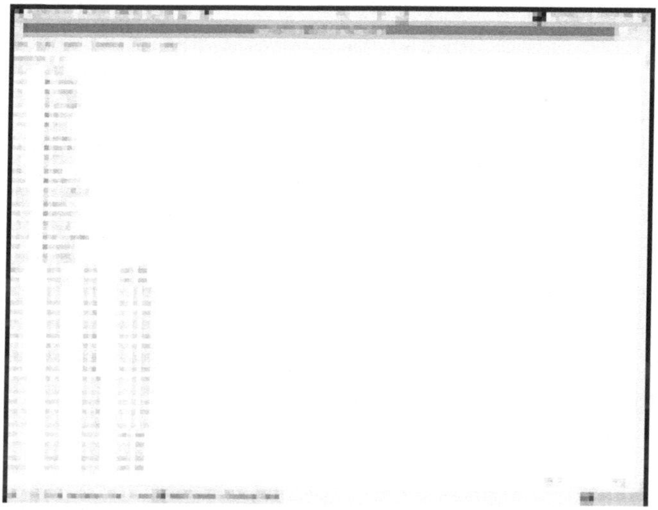

**Fig. 1.5 : Print-out—Network of Words formed between 12 Net Words**

The word net is represented in SLF, ie Standard Lattice Format in terms of nodes and arcs. Node represents word and arch represents link between words. In the current word net we have 120 words (including NULL words) and arcs among the word. Fig. 1.5 shows screen shot of sample file in Standard Lattice Format developed with 12 words network.

A statistical word net is formed by having words are as nodes and the link-log transition probability as the link between arcs.

### *F. Recognition*

HMM recognizer recognizes the words based on the language model (SLF) and acoustic model created by training set. Initially forced alignment is used to align the state of the testing utterance[5]. The Viterbi decoding algorithm matches the state with the trained states. At every step, P suitable states are selected among the different states of M models. Then it produces the sequence of the next many possible states.

Among those many possible states few highest probable states are chosen and so on. Likewise the lattice structure preceded and compared with the training pattern. For every possible state in every model the probability of observation is calculated. The overall probability of all possible states per model is multiplied. The model with the highest overall probability will be chosen as the resultant model (word) of utterance.

The word uttered is recognized based on Viterbi decoding techniques[8]. The HMM parameter of the state sequence of uttered word is generated and matched against the sequence of trained words as shown in the fig. 1.6. Many similar words have the higher probability and the word is labelled as label of word which has the nearest matching or has highest probability[5].

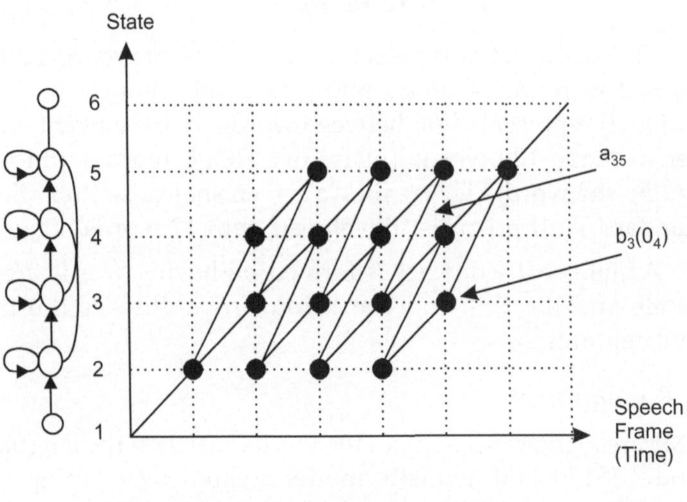


**Fig. 1.6 : Viterbi decoding algorithm IR Rabiner and B.H. Juang. Fundamentals Spech Recognition, Pearsan Education, 1993**

The probability of input belonging to different models are compared in Decision Logic. The model with highest score is the model of input observation.

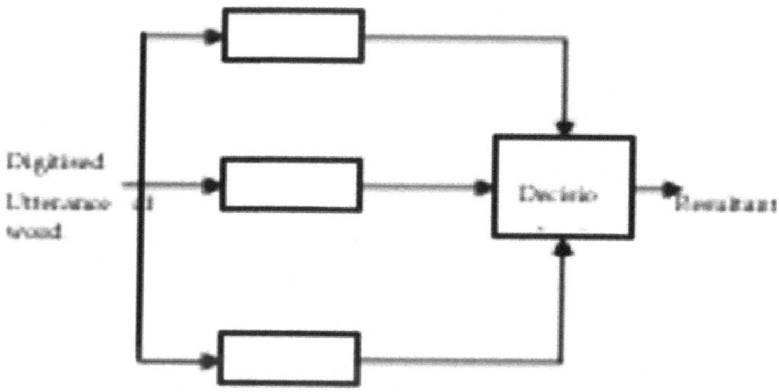

**Fig. 1.7 : HMM Model**

## Tamizh Tutoring System

The tamizh tutoring system is devised to enhance the tamizh learning interest amongst children. A Picture driven system along with audio attracts the children to learn tamizh language. It bridges the gap of lack of interest in learning with usual keyboard and mouse interface. Therefore there will definite impact in education system on this interactive tutoring.

This tutoring system has been developed with inputs from various theories of learning such as Bloom's Taxonomy[6]. According to it, the learning consists of three domains: Cognitive, Affective, and Pshycomotor skills. Cognitive learning is improving the mental ability (Informative, Recognizing and Recalling) – our system brings out cognitive skills by making the child to recognize an object, recall it. It addresses Affective skills (receiving, responding valuing, motivation and appreciation) by responding on her recognition. It also brings in Psychomotor skills (involve more physical activities) – by making the child to use microphone, mouse keyboard and speaker.

A picture of index one is displayed and a child is asked to name the picture. The child has to record the identity of object in his voice. The word is recorded and given as the input to speech engine. The speech engine produces the corresponding word in textual form. The word is mapped into index and matched against the index of the picture displayed. The matching module sends a signal to scoring system. The scoring system evaluates and pop out choice for next trial if needed The system gives maximum three choices per word to a child, if the child recognition is wrong or uttered the word with different pronunciation, the word is displayed to child in textual form and audio corresponds to the word is playing. On success, the system just display the object identity in text then system iterates through next picture till end. At the end of picture gallery the system displays score with the word of appreciation and continue till the child wish to quit. This system not only trains the oral pronunciation of word but also trains the object in written form. Figure 8 shows the screen shot of VBaTTS system.

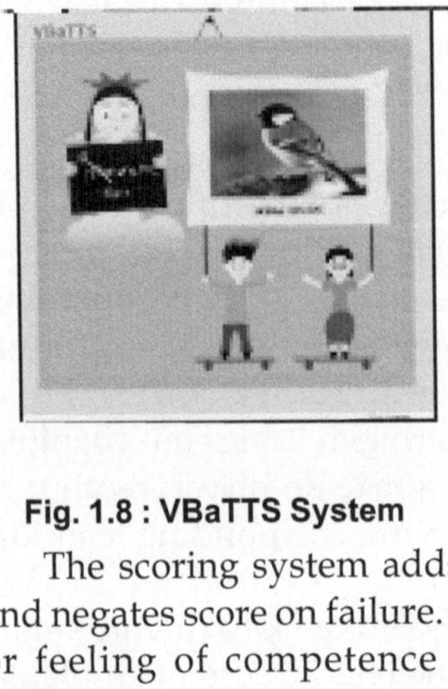

**Fig. 1.8 : VBaTTS System**

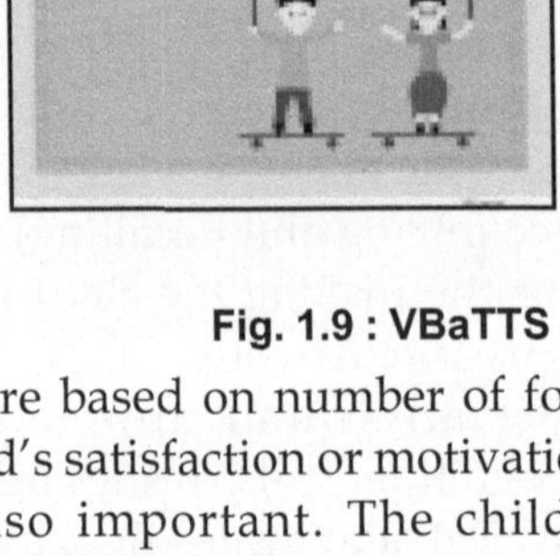

**Fig. 1.9 : VBaTTS**

The scoring system adds score based on number of foul and negates score on failure. Child's satisfaction or motivation or feeling of competence is also important. The child's achievement level is meaningless if the child chooses not to exercise the skill after acquiring it. Thus the system operates in different level and the score is displayed in grade if it is Excellent or very good else the system just says the score is not good enough and asks the child to reattempt.

## Conclusions and Scope for Future Work

The speech engine is not producing 100 per cent accuracy. To overcome this, system has to be enriched with speaker normalization and emotion normalization. The accuracy of the system also can be improved by adding some more parameter like speech rate and intensity etc to build the acoustic model of a word.

## Acknowledgement

We acknowledge Dr. T. Nagarajan, Professor and Head, Department of IT, SSN College of Engineering, Chennai, for his valuable guidance in developing speech engine. We also thank AICTE for funding a project on development of tamizh speech engine.

## REFERENCES

1. Ben Gold and Nelson Morgan, Speech and Audio Signal Processing, John Wiley and Sons Inc. , Singapore, 2004
2. LR.Rabiner and R.W.Schaffer Digital Processing of Speech Signals Prentice Hall—1978
3. Veenayagamoorthy, Viresh Kumar and Kumes Sadrasegaran Voice Recognition Using Neural Network in Science Direct—IEEE 1998
4. L.R.Rabiner and B.H.Juang, Fundamentals Speech Recognition, Pearson Education, 1993.
5. L.Rabiner A Tutorial on Hidden Markov Models and Selected Applications IEEE, Vol. 77 No. 2, 1989.
6. Benjamin S. Bloom Taxonomy of Educational Objectives, Handbook 1: Cognitive Domain ISBN-13: 9780582280106 Publisher: Addison Wesley Publishing Comp
7. M.Helander, T. K. Landauer, P. Prabhu (Eds) Intelligent Tutoring Systems—Handbook of Human-Computer Interaction, Second, Completely Revised Edition, Elsevier Science B. V., c1997, Chapter 37
8. Schultz, W.Black, Schultz,W.Black,Horynyak,Kominek, SPICE :Web Paged Tool for Rapid Language Adaptation in Speech Processing Systems, in the Proceedings of INTERSPEECH 2007

9. Krstulovic, S., Hunecke, A. and Schrder, M. (2007). An HMM-Based Speech Synthesis System Applied to German and Its Adaptation to a Limited Set of Expressive Football Announcements.Proc. Interspeech Antwerp, Belgium

10. Saraswathy, S., Geetha T.V. 2004. Building Language Models for Tamil Speech Recognition System. In Proceedings of AACC2004 and LNCS3285, 161-168

2

# Tamil Blogs
## *Tools, Aggregators and Beyond*

*— Kasi Arumugam*

**ABSTRACT**

*Evolution of Blogs in Tamil started in 2003 and is growing steadily. This chapter describes technical challenges faced by Tamil Bloggers at the early phase mainly caused by encoding related issues, and how Unicode got established as a standard for Tamil web. As founder-developer of the first Tamil blog aggregator Tamilmanam, the author explains the features and issues of tools and services dedicated for the Tamil Web Content Management with particular relevance to Blogs. By recording events, the chapter attempts to help future web development efforts targeted for Tamil community. A few thoughts on the current trends and future possibilities are also touched upon.*

## The Basics of Blogs

A Blog is a personal website that helps an individual or a team of few people to publish their content on the internet for many others to read. The fundamental differences between a typical 'website' and a blog (even though slowly getting blurred these days), can be explained by the following table:

| Feature | A typical 'Website' | A Blog |
|---|---|---|
| Updating frequency | Less frequent—some of these not updated since launch | Very frequent, sometimes several times a day |
| People involved | Autho→ Designer→ Developer→Publisher/ Hoster | Blogger |
| Run by | Institution/Business/ Government | Individuals |
| Real-world equivlents | Magazine, Newspaper, Brochure, Book, Directory, Album, etc. | Nothing exactly Closest is Handbill, Letters-to-the-editor, Manuscript magaine |
| Participation model | Readers have no direct say | Readers' participate through comments; bring life into the system |

## Evolution of Blogs as Alternative Media Around the World

Blog is a child of technology. Unlike other forms of publications that had a classical form and a modern form, blogs cannot be thought of without the 'wired world' that is today's World-Wide-Web. Blogs takes away the need for an author to be at the mercy of an editor or a publisher. Blogs have brought in equality and democracy to the countless minds that aim at the 'authorship'. Thus a blog makes the voices of weak and less-opportune people be heard—technology's true gift to the society.

Blogs have started playing vital roles, more visibly so in developed countries, in politics, technology and issues concerning societies. Leading media websites have exclusive pages to show popular blogs, e.g.

- New York Times – USA (http://www.nytimes.com/ref/topnews/blog-index.html)
- Guardian – UK (http://www.guardian.co.uk/tone/blog)
- The Indian Express – India (http://www.expressbuzz blogs.com/).
- BBC – UK (http://www.bbc.co.uk/blogs/)

## Technological Challenges Faced By early Tamil Bloggers

It is understandable that Blog authors need to have access to web-enabled computers. But, Tamil Bloggers were challenged by few more special needs: the authoring tools and displaying technologies.

They had three major needs:

1. Tamil typing tools for entering their writings into the computer, with facilities to convert from one encoding to another.
2. Technologies for ensuring that those prospective readers see Tamil text properly at their desktop without any downloads/modifying browser configurations.
3. Tamil typing tools for readers to enter comments using no new downloads/learning.

Technology enthusiasts and volunteer teams lent great help to Tamil Bloggers in this area that brought Tamil blogs to the forefront of many Indic languages.

## Tamil typing tools

While there were many tools available for typing Tamil in computers, the Tamil blogging community mainly operated with only few tools viz. Murasu Editor, e-Kalappai and PonguTamil writer. Murasu Systems offered free downloads of Murasu Editor. e-Kalappai was made a free download thanks to a group of donors who had paid on behalf of the community. PonguTamil was an online service from suratha.com. Of these, due to the simplicity and compatibility with multiple applications, e-Kalappai was the most popular among Bloggers, particularly those who entered Tamil computing after the blog era started. PonguTamil (http://www.suratha.com/reader.htm ) suited those without having rights to install anything on their computers.

## Display-Related Issues

Then came the next challenge. Hitherto, most websites displaying Tamil content had their text created with a variety of encodings. There were proprietary fonts every viewer needs to download and install for each website one visits. Even after this, there were browser settings one had to do in order to see Tamil properly rendered on their screen.

Unicode standard was already out and few websites like ezhilnila.com, thisaigal.com, etc. have been displaying Unicode Tamil content. This demonstrated that Unicode provided the answer to most of the issues concerning displaying text at reader's computer out-of-the-box—no font downloads any tricky browser settings. This sealed the growth of other encodings for Tamil Blogs. Even few blogs operating with TSCII text had to eventually convert to Unicode.

With the growth of blogs in Tamil, Unicode became the *de-facto* encoding standard for the Tamil web. Today the most visited media sites such as Dinamani, Dinamalar, Dinakaran, Kumudam, Vikatan etc., in Tamil are in Unicode.

## Windows 98—Specific Issues

Still there was a need to support the computers running on Windows 98, where Unicode was not working straight away. Users still needed to download Unicode fonts; People offered how-to help pages for enabling Indic language setting, updating the uniscribe rendering library (USP10.dll). But still it needed a simpler solution. The web embedded font technology (WEFT) of Microsoft (simply called 'dynamic font') filled in this gap and Tamil Bloggers readily grabbed it. Of course it required certain paid technology that worked only for a given domain. Thanks to Athirampattinam Umar Thambi's domainindependent dynamic font file Thenee.eot, Tamil blogs exploited this technology to the fullest extent and all their blogs were fully working in Windows 98. Thenee was such useful tool that it supported both TSCII and Unicode in a single font file, helping many comment-writers who were using TSCII as part of their Yahoo group activity.

## Tamil Typing Tools for Comment-writers

The last Tamil-specific challenge was to offer means for the blog readers to type-in their comments. Obviously it was utterly impractical to expect a casual reader to learn and install tools/settings for typing in Tamil. Being online tool running on JavaScript that every browser supported, PonguTamil JavaScript code was embedded into many comment boxes enabling Romanized input of Tamil by readers. Gopi improved this further and offered with many options at http://www.higopi.com /ucedit/Reuse.html

## Volunteering and Community Efforts

Tamil Blogs started appearing in the scene from early 2003. There were several online resources mainly by early volunteers like Suratha Yazhvanan, Mathy Kandasamy, Umar Thambi, etc. explaining blogging in general and Tamil-specific issues in particular. These offered help and guidance for many early Bloggers. The 'Tamil Bloggers List' at http://

tamilblogs.blogspot.com/ originally compiled by Mathy Kandasamy was the launch pad for many new Bloggers. Community blog Valaippoo (http://valaippoo. blogspot.com/) was a a meeting point for discussing blogging related issues while its weekly authors tried to show case interesting posts from Tamil blogs. An article series by the author himself on essentials of blogging was originally published in e-sangamam e-zine and is still available at his personal blog at http://kasilingam.com/wiki/doku.php?id=tamil_blogging.

## Arrival of Aggregators

Having created and published their blog, the authors now had to overcome the next challenge: how to make themselves visible in the crowd? Unlike the conventional magazines, blogs are written with no fixed release day or time. Blog's ability to totally break the order of time needs a technological answer too. They need to keep the interested audience to know 'What is written fresh this minute? How to reach it? Who wrote it and who are all engaged in conversations on such stuff?'

Blog aggregators help answer the above questions through intelligent use of technology.www.tamilmanam.net (formerly www.thamizmanam.com, started in Aug 2004) was the first and foremost of the new genre of websites called blog aggregators. Tamil led the whole of India in the concept of blog aggregators and have pioneering efforts in this front. Blog aggregators resemble large communities on the cyberspace serving both authors and readers. They are the main streets of the blogging village and provide a meeting point; they make this momentum to sustain. Aggregators accelerate the pace of blogging movement thus plays a vital role in the growth of web pages in languages of the people.

## Blog Portal Tamilmanam

Using open source feed aggregation technology as its starting point for Tamilmanam, the author ventured into developing programs and services tailored to meet the specific needs of

Tamil bloggers. Tamilmanam employed the popular open-source tools PHP & MySQL to offer a feature-rich, contemporary service for the benefit of Tamil Bloggers.

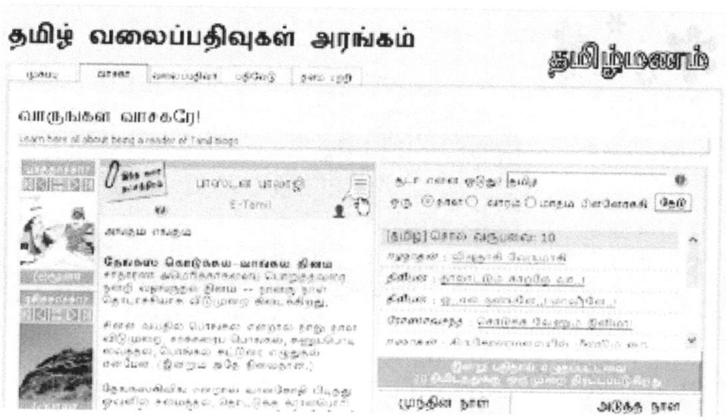


Some of the pioneering features of Tamilmanam were:

1. Bloggers List sortable by name, location, start date, etc. updated by auto submission of URL
2. Auto aggregation of posts (updated every 20 minutes)
3. Posts written in the past days
4. Posts written on specific topics/ genre
5. Automatic aggregation of Comment status
6. Facility to convert a post into a PDF document
7. Voting on posts
8. Automatic hiding of Non-Tamil post
9. Intimation of objectionable content

Tamilmanam's most visited 'readers' page w/star of the week, hot tags, auto-updated thumbnails of cartoons and photos - Nov-2004 Tamilmanam Star of the week showcased prominent Bloggers for a week.

Tamilmanam was the first to aggregate comments to blogs long before blogging services offered newsfeeds for comments. Tamil Blogs grew leaps and bounds with Tamilmanam. Chart given below published in one of the studies of blogs in India revealed the position of Tamil Blogs among other Indian language blogs.

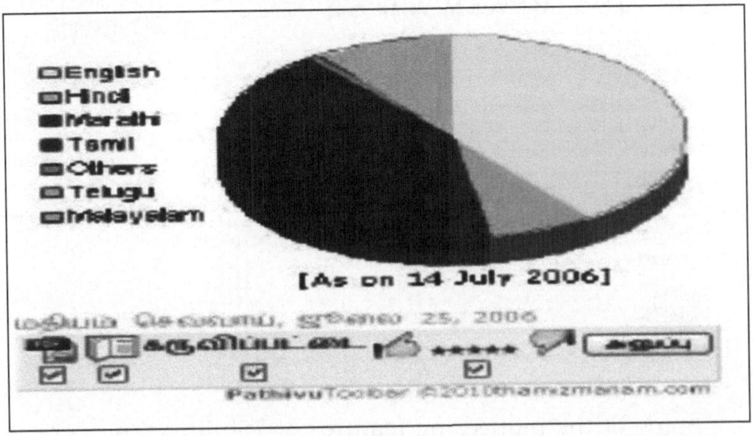


More than a year later, Tamilmanam was rewritten and upgraded to version 2 with Pathivu toolbar. This provided for instant aggregation, post-wise categorization, one-click voting and on-the-fly pdf ebook creation was first-of-its-kind technological feature of Tamilmanam.

## More Tamil Blog Aggregation Services

Thenkoodu was another aggregator service started around the time Tamilmanam v2 was launched but had to suspend operations due to sudden demise of the developer-owner, Sakaran. Other leading aggregator services Tamilveli and Thiratti are playing important roles in their own ways to further the growth of Tamil blogs.

Other than aggregators based on automated scripts, there were efforts by teams in showcasing select blog posts by manual recommendations. Gilli was a pioneering effort followed by Maatru. Tamilish merged the automation and manual recommendations using Digg.com model. There is a spurt of new aggregators coming out recently.

### Efforts Beyond Aggregation

Tamilmanam's efforts towards nurturing the alternative media and supporting Tamil computing was taken further by the current team TMI (Tamil Media International Inc), a US-registered non-profit organization. TMI team also brought out Poonga, a monthly e-zine based on collections entirely out of blog posts. TMI instituted an elaborate awards program for Tamil Blogs and have developed dedicated software for managing the award program that is unique in several ways, like there is no judges panel,etc.

### Tamilmanam Today

Tamilmanam currently aggregates over 7000 blogs that update with some 300+ posts everyday. It is feature-rich service and empowers a vibrant community of Tamil Bloggers. Many TMI members are part of INFITT and are involved in advancement of Tamil in internet and computing. Thanks to its primary technical contributor Sasikumar's continuous efforts, Tamilmanam is up-to-date in terms of technology. It is one of the few successful team efforts in Tamil computing world.

### Tamil Blogs as Alternative Media

The emergence of blogs has created an independent alternative media that touch upon issues hitherto not given adequate space. The speed, economy, varieties of topics and plural perspectives possible to be written in blogs have no parallels in the conventional media. Along with blogs, the language computing is coming of age and blogs are here to stay.

Many mainstream writers have started to blog. People from other creative fields, like the film world are also attracted towards this interesting and creative pastime. Many magazines have started highlighting interesting blogs. Some of the noted blogs have been printed into books too. All this lead to greater visibility for Tamil blogs that are showing signs of alternative media.

## The Trends of Tamil Bloggers

The micro-blogging service Twitter is an effective short communication-cum-networking medium that many Bloggers are now tweeters too. The companionship they have generated through their blogs helps them get a ready-made following in Twitter. Twitter is available in cell phones, a major push over other web-only networking services. Still, for expressing elaborate thoughts on the net, Tweeters use blogs.

There are several automated cross-service applications that lets one makes best use of each from the other. Many Bloggers trans-locate their friendship network into Social Networking such as FaceBook, Orkut, MySpace, etc. and Professional Networking such as LinkedIn. As in micro-blogging, their Blogging continues, albeit less frequently. Bloggers arrange meets as an extension of their coming together in Blogosphere. Such meetings of Tamil Bloggers are very common in Chennai, as here is the largest congregation of Tamil Bloggers. Meets also happen at locations such as Coimbatore, Puducherry, Bangalore, Erode, Madurai. Bloggers from the Diaspora too meet at Singapore, USA, UAE, Sri Lanka, etc. Bloggers organize workshops to encourage and help more would-be bloggers.

## Future Scenario

There are blog-driven news/media sites in English, a very popular one being SlashDot (www.slashdot.com ) Tamil blogs have full potential to evolve into such a format which will differ from plain aggregators/bookmarking applications. A possible blog-driven media site with following working arrangement is very much a reality:

1. Enlisted authors write independently and publish their articles at a central site on topical matters on a continuous basis.
2. Editor's panel is just to monitor and intervene on legal issues or complaints but no formal prereading before publication. This ensures timely publication on news and articles, but still moderated for integrity/legality.
3. This online media will have at a given time 10's or 100s of contributors, who have been selected by the editor's panel based on their demonstrated authorship. Thus there is no scope for much noise that is common in current aggregators.
4. There will be moderation of comments, voting and abuse-reporting
5. This site will be monetized by advertisements and the revenue will be shared among the contributors after deducting the expenses, proportional to the page hits of each article. Tamil blog world is waiting for web application developers to bring out interesting relevant applications.

# 3

# Prototype for e-Government Issued e-Card Using RFID Technology Based on Tamil Font Database

— *Vijayalakshmi, S.R.*

**ABSTRACT**

*RFID is not a new technology and has passed through many decades of use in military, airline, library, security, healthcare, sports, animal farms and other areas. Industries use RFID for various applications such as personal/vehicle access control, departmental store security, equipment tracking, baggage, fast food establishments, logistics, etc. The enhancement in RFID technology has brought advantages that are related to resource optimization, increased efficiency within business processes, and enhanced customer care, overall improvements in business operations and healthcare. Passports and other identification documents may be enhanced using the advancements in RFID technology. Various national and international bodies are pursuing machine-readable approaches with biometric information. This chapter examines implementation regarding these electronic approaches and developments toward electronic data storage and transmission. Radio-frequency identification (RFID) devices for electronic passports and other existing identity documents are discussed. Our proposed research aim is to produce a model for e-government. All identity information about the citizen is included and database is maintained in Tamil language. Every citizen is having voter ID, PAN card, Credit card, ration card, driving Licence information, insurance information, Passport and many more. All cards can be replaced with single e-Card. In the proposed model, database (all information about the citizen) is stored in tamil font using php mySQl database. This e-Card provided by the government could be used by the citizen. The E-government maintains database in Tamil of all citizens. It helps in identifying the person during voting time. It can be used as security. However, the focus of this chapter is to explore the main RFID components, i.e. the tag, antenna and reader.*

***Keywords:*** *RFID technology, Electronic Passport, e-Card, Biometrics.*

## Introduction

RFID stands for Radio Frequency Identification and is a term that describes a system of identification. RFID is based on storing and remotely retrieving information or data as it consists of RFID tag, RFID reader and back-end Database. RFID tags store unique identification information of objects and communicate the tags so as to allow remote retrieval of their ID. RFID technology depends on the communication between the RFID tags and RFID readers. The range of the reader is dependent upon its operational frequency. Usually the readers have their own software running on their ROM and also, communicate with other software to manipulate these unique identified tags. Basically, the application which manipulates tag deduction information for the end user, communicates with the RFID reader to get the tag information through antennas. Many researchers have addressed issues that are related to RFID reliability and capability. RFID is continuing to become popular because it increases efficiency and provides better service to stakeholders. RFID technology has been realized as a performance differentiator for a variety of commercial applications, but its capability is yet to be fully utilized.

## RFID Evolution

RFID technology has passed through many phases over the last few decades. The technology has been used in tracking delivery of goods, in courier services and in baggage handling. Other applications includes automatic toll payments, departmental access control in large buildings, personal and vehicle control in a particular area, security of items which shouldn't leave the area, equipment tracking in engineering firms, hospital filing systems, etc.

## How RFID System Works

Most RFID systems consist of tags that are attached to the objects to be identified. Each tag has its own 'read-only' or "rewrite" internal memory depending on the type and application. Typical configuration of this memory is to store product information, such as an object's unique ID personal details, etc. The RFID reader generates magnetic fields that enable the RFID system to locate objects (via the tags) that are within its range. The high-frequency electromagnetic energy and query signal generated by the reader triggers the tags to reply to the query; the query frequency could be up to 50 times per second. As a result communication between the main components of the system i.e. tags and reader is established.

If the reader is on and the tag arrives in the reader fields, then it automatically wakes-up and decodes the signal and replies to the reader by modulating the reader's field. All the tags in the reader range may reply at the same time, in this case the reader must detect signal collision (indication of multiple tags). Signal collision is resolved by applying anti-collision algorithm which enables the reader to sort tags and select/handle each tag based on the frequency range (between 50 tags to 200 tags) and the protocol used. In this connection the reader can perform certain operations on the tags such as reading the tag's identifier number and writing data into a tag. The reader performs these operations one by one on each tag.

## Components of an RFID System

This RFID system allows to deduct the objects (tag) and perform various operations on it. The integration of RFID components enables the implementation of an RFID solution. The RFID system consists of following five components (as shown in Figure 3.1):

- Tag (attached with an object, unique identification).
- Antenna (tag detector, creates magnetic field).
- Reader (receiver of tag information, manipulator).
- Communication infrastructure (enable reader/RFID to work through IT infrastructure).
- Application software (user database/application/interface).

### Tags

Tags contain microchips that store the unique identification (ID) of each object. The ID is a serial number stored in the RFID memory. The chip is made up of integrated circuit and embedded in a silicon chip. RFID memory chip can be permanent or changeable depending on the read/write characteristics. Read-only and rewrite circuits are different as read-only tag contains fixed data and can not be changed without re-program electronically. On the other hand, re-write tags can be programmed through the reader at any time without any limit. For example, in the case of the credit cards, small plastic peaces are stuck on various objects, and the labels. Labels are also embedded in a variety of objects such as documents, cloths, manufacturing materials etc.

There are two types of tags (active and passive) are being used by industry and most of the RFID system. The essential characteristics of RFID tags are their function to the RFID system. This is based on their range, frequency, memory, security, type of data and other characteristics. These characteristics are core for RFID performance and differ in usefulness/support to the RFID system operations.

### *Tag Frequencies*

The range of the RFID tags depends on their frequency. This frequency determines the resistance to interference and other performance attributes. The use/selection of RFID tag depends on the application; different frequencies are used on different RFID tags. The following are the commonly used frequencies:

***Microwave*** works on 2.45 GHz, it has good reader rate even faster than UHF tags. Although at this frequency the reading rate results are not the same on wet surfaces and near metals, the frequency produce better results in applications such as vehicle tracking (in and out with barriers), with approximately 1 meter of tags read range.

***Ultra High Frequency*** works within a range of 860-930 MHz, it can identify large numbers of tags at one time with quick multiple read rate at a given time. So, it has a considerable good reading speed. It has the same limitation as Microwave when is applied on wet surface and near metal. However, it is faster than high frequency data transfer with a reading range of 3 meters.

***High Frequency*** works on 13.56MHz and has less than one meter reading range but is inexpensive and useful for access control, items identifications on sales points etc as it can implanted inside thin things such as paper.

***Low Frequency*** works on 125 kHz, it has approximately half a meter reading range and mostly used for short reading range applications.

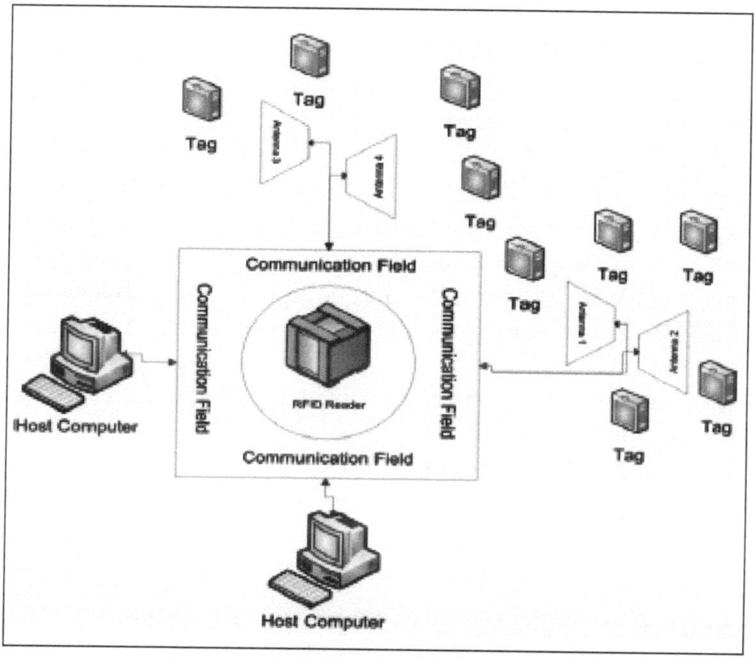


**Fig. 3.1 : Components of an RFID System**

## Antennas

RFID antennas collect data and are used as a medium for tag reading. It consists of the following: (*i*) Patch antennas; (*ii*) Gate antennas; (*iii*) Linear polarized; (*iv*) Circular polarized; (*v*) Di-pole or multipole antennas; (*vi*) Stick antennas; (*vii*) Beam-forming or phased-array element antennas; (*viii*) Adaptive antennas; and (*ix*) Omni directional antennas.

## RFID Reader

RFID reader works as a central place for the RFID system. It reads tags data through the RFID antennas at a certain frequency. Basically, the reader is an electronic apparatus which produce and accept a radio signals. The antennas contains an attached reader, the reader translates the tags radio signals through antenna, depending on the tags capacity. The readers consist of a build-in anticollision schemes and a single reader can operate on multiple frequencies. As a result, these readers are expected to collect or write data onto tag (in case) and pass to computer systems. For this purpose readers can be connected using RS-232, RS-485, USB cable as a wired options (called serial readers) and connect to the computer system. Also can use WiFi as wireless options which also known as network readers. Readers are electronic devices which can be used as standalone or be integrated with other devices and the following components/hardware into it: (*i*) Power for running reader; (*ii*) Communication interface; (*iii*) Microprocessor; (*iv*) Channels; (*v*) Controller; (*vi*) Receiver; (*vii*) Transmitter; and (*viii*) Memory.

## Storing Tamil Font Using PHP

By default mysql supports many european languages, Since unicode character (UTF-8) support implemented in mysql it allows us to store many of the indian (Asian) languages.Mysql supports Gujrathi, Hindi, Telugu and TAMIL among too many languages in the subcontinent. Let's consider TAMIL language and workout.To store & search tamil character sets in MySQL table, first of all we need to create a table with character set UTF-8.

## Conclusion

This study has identified and explained the nature of RFID technology evolution with respect to RFID applications. RFID technology will open new doors to make organizations, companies more secure, reliable, and accurate. The first part of this chapter has explained and described the RFID technology and its components, and the second part has discussed the main considerations of Tamil font in the PHP my SQL. The chapter considers RFID technology as a means to provide new capabilities and efficient methods for e-Governance. The implementation of e-Card has not been without challenges, and some continue to challenge the use of contactless technology and other identity documents. This paper analyzed the major current and potential uses of RFID in identity documents. This chapter also gave a model for e-Card using RFID technology and E-card information could be stored in the tamil font databse.

## REFERENCES


1. Yingjiu Li, Member, Vipin Swarup, and Sushil Jajodia, Fingerprinting Relational Databases:Schemes and Specialties *IEEE, IEEE Transactions on Dependable and Secure Computing*, Vol. 2, No. 1, January-March 2005 pp. 34 to 45.
2. S. Garfinkel, B. Rosenberg, "*RFID Application, Security, and Privacy*", USA, (2005), ISBN: 0- 321-29096-8.
3. L. Srivastava, *RFID: Technology, Applications and Policy Implications*, Presentation, International Telecommunication Union, Kenya, (2005).
4. A. Narayanan, S. Singh and M. Somasekharan, "*Implementing RFID in Library: Methodologies, Advantages and Disadvantages*", (2005).
5. S. Shepard, (2005), "*RFID Radio Frequency Identification*", (2005), USA, ISBN:0-07-144299-5.

4

# Recommended Approach for e-Governance in Tamil Nadu Using MPMLA.IN

— *Syed Hussain*

## Core Objective

The topic of this presentation is based on my experiences with MPMLA.IN website http://mpmla.in/. The objective is to present this working model as a sample way to implement eGovernance using a mixture of technologies related to Tamil language to help the elected representatives to interact with general public and also to use it to effectively improve the quality of life of common man.

## Current Implementation and Limitations

Currently, MPMLA.IN covers all the MPs and MLAs in every single parliamentary and assembly constituency in India. The website is an unbiased effort to facilitate communication between people and their respective MPs/MLAs in India. The people can put across their grievance/appreciation to their MP/MLA and the MP/MLA can choose to respond and address the issue. There is no bias or political affiliation.

### Key Features

Some of the key features available for the visitors to MPMLA.IN today are:

- Easy identification of MPs and MLAs from the website by State, Parliamentary Constituency and Assembly Constituency.
- Search by MP, MLA, Party, Constituency or Politician.
- Easy entry of problems using English language as well as typing in English automatically converted to Tamil.
- Every feedback and problem reported is validated by moderators before publishing on the site.
- Top Five Issues List: A Top Five Issues list is available across each constituency thus helping the elected representatives to focus on the core problems reported in their constituency.

### Major Limitations

Some of the main limitations we identified are:

- People who are not comfortable in English are forced to express their thoughts in English.
- People who know English and Tamil try to type in Tamil language using English alphabets.
- People who only know Tamil cannot express their concerns on the website
- People who do not have a computer cannot express their concerns

The idea behind this chapter is to recommend an enhanced version of MPMLA.IN as a viable model for e-Governance using various technology advances in Tamil. This model also addresses the major limitations mentioned above, along with many additional features. The following page has a screen shot of how MPMLA.IN looks today. This is followed by sections explaining the new technology advancements recommended in the near future and also the long term plan for the same.

Screen shot of MPMLA.IN website as of 14-Apr-2010

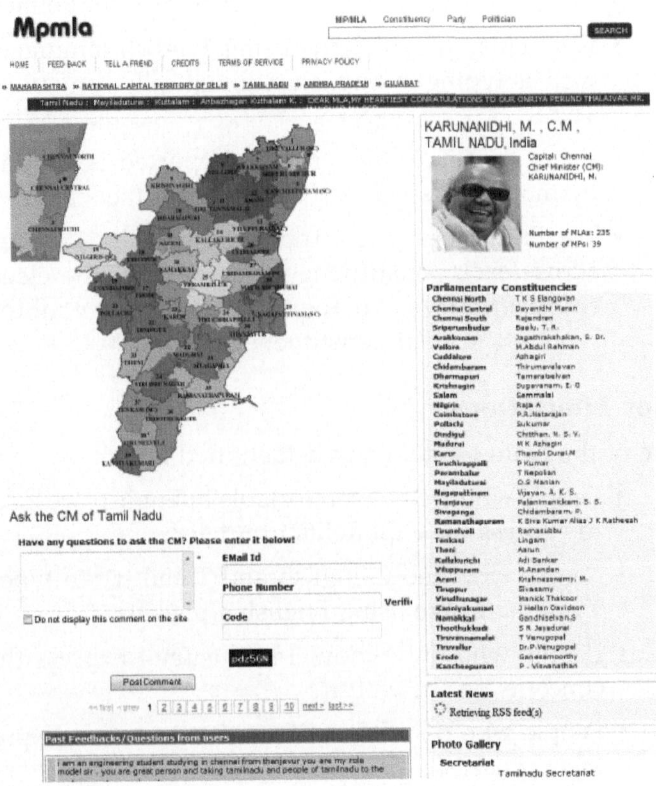


## Planned Implementation for eGovernance Using MPMLA.IN

The following section gives a full scope of how the existing model can be adopted in Tamil Nadu by leveraging technology advancements in Tamil.

## Overview

MPMLA.IN can be adopted by Government of Tamil Nadu as the central system for general public to report and track their day to day non-emergency issues. This system will facilitate better tracking and monitoring of any problem across the state.

The following are some of the core features to be integrated in the immediate future in MPMLA.IN

## Elected Official Login Management

- *Main Login Module*: Every elected official will be able to access the problems reported by the visitors using various methods such as computer, mobile devices, etc.
- *Communication Module*: The elected official can use this method to communicate their thoughts and ideas over a period of time.
- *Delegation*: Elected officials can also delegate their access to their subordinates—this way they do not have to always be present to type all the responses. The responses can be typed up by the delegates and submitted. This also makes it easy for the elected representative to quickly give follow-ups based on each issue.

## Problem Management Process

- Feedback and Problem Submission
- *Computer*—Typing in Tamil or English—Any one can access the MPMLA.IN website and type their problem in Tamil or English and report the issue.
- *SMS*—in Tamil or English—Any person can SMS their issues to a number from their mobile device.
- *Voice Mail*—in Tamil or English—The system allows users to call a toll free number and record their

messages. This message will be automatically converted into text using a voice to text software.

- *Picture*—Users of the system can also choose to upload any photo that represents a problem better. For eg. If a road is in a poor condition, a visitor can take a photo and upload it from their mobile device or from a computer. This image will be associated with the problem mentioned by the visitor.

## Problem Command Centre

A Problem Command Centre has to be established in order to review, analyse and also route the problem to its right officials. The Problem Command Centre also takes care of the following items:

## Feedback Parsing

Every feedback is automatically parsed and allocated based on the following parameters:

- MP or MLA under whom the problem was reported
- Area under which the problem was reported
- Nature of the issue (eg. Road, Water, etc)

## Problem Number Allocation

Every feedback identified as a problem is allocated a unique Problem Number and tracked on the website. This Number helps track every issue from initiation to closure.

**Service Level Agreement (SLA)** with Escalation Procedure

- SLA Time commitment: Every elected representative will commit to a specific time within which an issue will be replied to. This commitment will be officially displayed on the site and communicated to the problem reporter. Whenever a reply is made by any official, it will include the following:

- The current status of the issue
- Description of what has been done so far and what is planned
- When will the next update be provided on this issue
- Escalation Procedure: A well defined escalation procedure will be implemented in place which says who will be contacted if a person does not respond on time. This will make sure that if the issue crosses its SLA time, it will be escalated to the next higher official up in the chain of command. This will continue until the problem is addressed and resolved.

## Periodic Analysis and Reporting

### *Dashboards*

The plan is to provide extensive dashboard for each constituency so that the entire details about each issue are available at any time to any one visiting the constituency page. This also helps each official to understand key issues, their categories, etc

### *Reports*

Various reports will be generated to show problems that are unattended for a long time, repeated patterns, etc. This can be generated for any given time period, thus helping us to understand the history of an issue and identify repeatable pattern of issues, so that we can find a permanent fix for the same.

### *Comparison Charts*

Comparison Charts help us to understand how one constituency is handled with respect to another and how each elected official has performed over a period of time. This kind of metrics provides competitive analysis, based on which we can even arrive at the Constituency Index which will help us determine how a constituency fares in comparison to a similar constituency anywhere else in India.

### *Benefits for Elected Representatives*

- *Additional Communication Medium*: This platform provides the elected representative an additional communication medium to interact with the citizens.
- *Transparent View of Status*: This platform provides the responsible officials with a full view of all the issues, their status and also how they are performing when compared to their peers.

### *Benefits for Citizens*

- *Suggestion Box at Home*: People do not have to leave their homes and can directly report the feedback or issues using their computer or their cell phones.
- *Transparency and Accountability*: This model gives complete transparency on each issue reported by the people. This also improves the accountability on the part of the officials as they are aware that their performance is tracked publicly by every one.
- *Social Awareness and Involvement*: This form of interaction will automatically improve social awareness and improve the level of involvement for citizens in contributing towards improving their areas.

## Future Enhancements

### *All Elected Representatives*

One way of expanding MPMLA.IN would be to include the elected representatives at all levels starting from local municipality elections. This way every single elected representative will be able to have a full scope of their local issues as well as how it rolls up under the larger platform. This also provides full transparency and accountability at all levels.

## All Government Officials

A second way of expanding MPMLA.IN would be to include all the Government officials belonging to various departments such as Public Works, Transportation, Industries and Commerce, etc. This will make sure there is complete transparency across all the departments that handle the day to day affairs of the people.

## Conclusion

This approach is recommended to provide the simplest approach for any one in Tamil Nadu to leverage this system in order to have better reach to their elected representatives. A proper execution of this plan will ensure that there is better progress in every single area where there is a lack of attention today—thus leveraging various technologies to solve day to day problems for the common public.

## REFERENCES

1. Election Commission of India Website
2. Google Maps
3. Google Transliteration Tool
4. Vlingo Speech to Text Software
5. Elgg Social Networking Software

# 5

# e-Governance Initiatives in Tamil Nadu

*— E. Iniya Nehru*

E-governance Initiatives have resulted in improving core infrastructure and providing better services to citizens. IT has come a long way in changing the lives of the common man at the grassroot level. National Informatics Centre has been providing informatics support to Central Ministries, State Government and District Administration. It has gained deep understanding of governance issues which have paved way for successful designing and implementation of many e-Governance projects like Land Records, Registration, AGMARKNET, Examination Results, e-Post, Passport etc. The impact of government initiatives has been observed in all sectors i.e. administration, agriculture, rural development, judiciary, health, education, telecommunication and transport. In Tamil Nadu, the major e-Governance projects implemented are explained in detail.

**Tamil Nilam**

Tamil Nadu Infosystem on Land Administration and

Management (Tamil NILAM) is a major e-Governance initiative taken by the Revenue Department of Government of Tamil Nadu. This software system is developed to computerise the Land Records System in Tamil Nadu. Tamil Nilam is currently implemented in all the rural taluks in the State. It handles all the transactions relating to Land Records in the State.

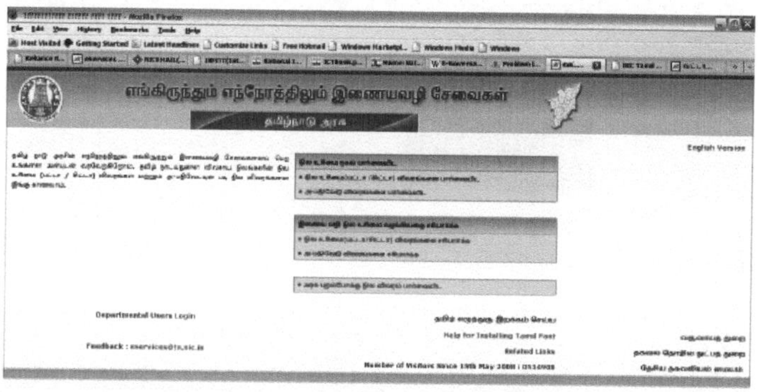


### *Objectives of Tamil NILAM*

- Delivery of all possible Citizen-centric e-services
- The entire contents are in TAMIL
- Issue of Chitta Extract (Record of Right)/A Register Extract/Adangal Extract to citizens
- Creation of Master database storing plot-wise and owner-wise details of land, crop, revenue, etc
- Generation of periodic reports through the computerized system.
- Improved and efficient service
- Easy maintenance and updates of Land Records
- Transparent administration
- Availability of information to public through Touch Screen Kiosk
- Exchange of data to other departments such as Sub Registrar Office, Agriculture Department etc.

## Vahan and Sarathi

Vahan and Sarathi are application Software developed for State Transport Authority, Tamil Nadu.

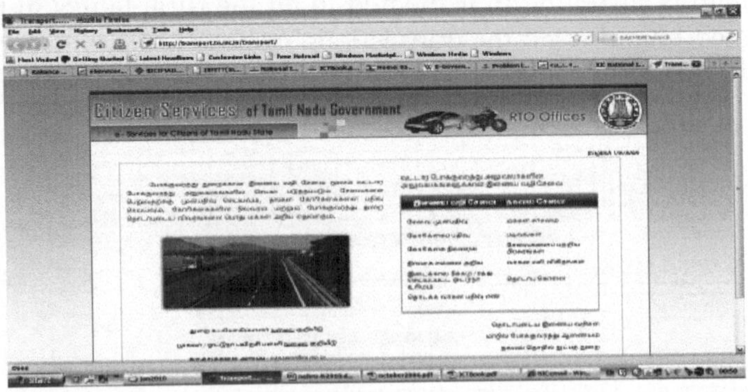


*Vahan* is for processing all transactions related to Vehicles and *Sarathi* is for processing Driving Licence and related activities. Vahan can be used to issue of Registration Certificate and Permits. Sarathi can be used to issue a Learners Licence, Permanent Driving Licence, Conductor Licence and also Driving School Licence to the applicant. The system was implemented on pilot basis in in RTO Chennai (North). The system was then approved for implementation in all other RTOs in Tamil Nadu. The systems have now been implemented in 71 offices.

## *Registration Department (STAR)*

Property Registration STAR (Simplified and Transparent Administration of Registration) is implemented in 450 Sub-Registrar Offices. Guideline Values of more than 2 crore Survey Subdivisions are hosted on Internet for public access. The system has enabled citizens to apply for Encumbrance Certificate online. The registration details are maintained in Tamil. The Sub-Registrar Offices and Taluk Offices in 40 taluks are connected using LAN for sharing the data of each other.

## Employment Online

The Professional Employment Exchange Office (PEEO) caters to the employment needs of professionals registered in Tamil Nadu for the entire state. The PEEO office comes under the Directorate of Employment and Training, registers the candidates seeking employment opportunities and recommends to various departments / offices requesting suitable professionals. The PEEO has decided to open their databases for access to the private sector employers, to create more avenues for the registered candidates. The mushrooming growth of private sector employment in this information era necessitates to make online web access of the entire database of registered candidates. In this scenario, the department has created a online web portal for the welfare of candidates and thrown open the entire online database for private sector employment opportunities. The website is operational from June 2003.

### *The objectives of this web site are as follows*

- To develop a Data Bank of highly qualified, marketable candidates from the Live Register of the Employment Exchanges in Tamil Nadu with the accent on persons with professional, executive and engineering diploma and degrees.
- To allow the private sector employers easy access to this database to fill up vacancies arising in their establishments and to offer facilities for screening and short-listing of prospective employees.
- To provide online information on application deadlines, track careers and future trends in employment.

### *Intra Management Information System Portal for Tamil Nadu Pollution Control Board (TNPCB)*

This Intranet based Monitoring System has been implemented to create database on all types of Industries (Profiles), the

Consents Details and Hazardous Waste Authorisation Details of various types of Industries in Tamil Nadu. This web application is used as an efficient Monitoring System by TNPCB Corporate Office, Chennai. Different types of MIS Reports are being generated using this IntraMIS both at State and District levels. Each TNPCB District Office updates AIR and WATER Pollution related data for all the Industries (taken from the 'Application for Consent' submitted by these Industries under Central Act 14 of 1981) functioning in its Jurisdiction. Each industry is identified by a unique File Number assigned by the respective TNPCB District Office. Industry Profile Data, Consents related data and Hazardous Waste related data are being captured for each industry using this web application.

### *e-Karuvoolam: Automated Treasury Bill Passing System*

Automated Treasury Bill Passing System (e-Karuvoolam) is aimed at automating the existing manual billing system of Treasury Department.The Workflow based Systems developed for the Treasury Department, enables to capturing the data starting from bill submission stage at the counters. Treasury is the "Bank of Government", functioning with the objective of maintaining all transactions to the government and sending reports to the Accountant General. Any transaction related to government is performed in the form of a bill. Initially a bill is submitted to the counter of a Sub Treasury / District Treasury / Pay and Accounts Office through a messenger. The bill goes through a phase of approval. This phase is called auditing the bill. Auditing clerk can reject the bill or can approve the bill. If the bill is approved, it is sent to the cheque release counter. The clerks at cheque release counter handover the cheque to the messenger if Treasury type is banking. The application software developed by NIC provides online environment with systems available on all working tables starting from the bill submission counter. The officials can process the bills online and take action for passing / rejecting the claim.

### *e-Governance at Madras High Court*

Systems in use at Madras High Court deals with

- Posting of Case Status of Madras High Court on Internet
- Display systems are installed at principal bench and Madurai bench to know the status of cases being heard at court halls. 35 court hall display and 6 composite display are installed at Principal bench.
- Certified copies of Final orders, Bails/Anticipatory Bails and interim application orders are entered and issued through the system. The computerized system has reduced the time delay in issuance of copies to the litigants. The Interim application orders are issued through the system since 26th Feb 2001.
- Systems for posting Case Status have been developed. The case details have been hosted on Internet.
- Interactive Voice Response System is installed at Madras High Court to know the Case Status through telephone.
- Touch Screen Kiosk is installed at Madras High Court for public dissemination.
- Daily Cause Lists are being prepared using the system. Systems are installed at Filing Countre, Posting sections for preparation of cause list.
- Daily Cause Lists are being hosted on Internet. Number of hits per day is more than 7000 on working days. As per the statistics available, Madras HC is receiving maximum number of hits.
- Reported Judgements are being hosted on Internet. More than 1500 users visit the Madras HC Judgement site every day.

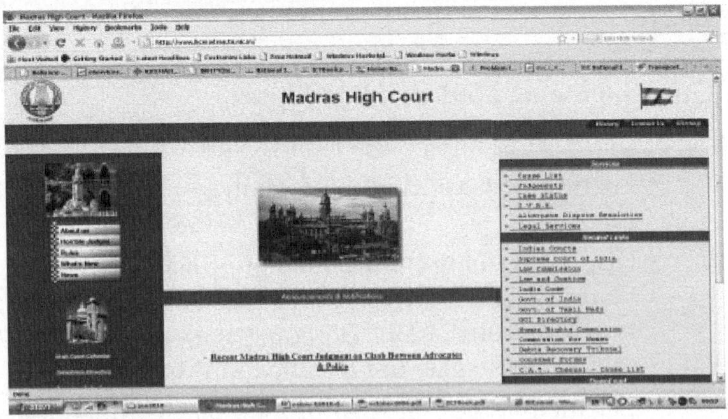


- Statistical reports relating to disposed cases statements are prepared regularly.
- Information Centre functions at Madras High Court for the benefit of Litigant public to know the status of cases filed at Madras HC. Around 700 case enquiries are received at the enquiry counter every day.

### *e-Attendance Monitoring System*

This Application is being used by the 'e-Governance Cell' of the DoTE, to monitor the Attendance Details of about 2.71 Lakhs Diploma Students studying in about 340 Polytechnic Institutions all over the State. Monthly Attendance details of every student are to be entered by the respective Institution in the first week of the following month. Duly signed hard copies of the Branch-wise Attendance Registers are to be generated from this application and to be sent to DoTE for filing purposes. Any time, a student can login to view his/her Attendance Details for the current Academic Year. At the end of the semester, Hall Tickets will be generated only for the Eligible Students taken from this e- Attendance Database. Thus this Intranet application helps the DoTE to streamline and to bring transparency to the Examination Processing System in the DoTE.

### Single Window Counseling System

This system has been implemented for admissions to more than 390 Teacher Training Institutes in the State.

### Common Integrated Police Administration

The CIPA software is designed and developed to maintain the details pertaining to all the activities of the Police Stations relating to Crime and Criminals. The system provides required information to the higher levels periodically and as and when required. The system also generates various statutory reports for the smooth functioning of the police station. The ultimate goal of the computerization would be an integrated networked system with state of the art hardware and software in place for police access and use the Information in their day to day work and to take decisions. The software is a total work-flow system having the following three major modules along with reports and queries viz., Registration, Investigation and Prosecution.

### Agricultural Marketing Information System Network (AGMARKNET)

The **AGMARKNET** project is sponsored by Directorate of Marketing and Inspection (DMI), Ministry of Agriculture, and implemented by National Informatics Centre. It aims to link all Regulated Markets, State Agricultural marketing Boards / Directorates and DMI regional offices located throughout the country, for effective information exchange on market prices.

The **AGMARKNET** website (www.agmarknet.nic.in) is a G2C e-governance portal and available in Tamil for the markets in Tamil Nadu, caters to the needs of various stakeholders such as farmers, industry, policy makers and academic institutions by providing agricultural marketing related information from a single window. It facilitates dissemination, over web, of the daily arrivals and prices of commodities in the agricultural produce markets spread across the country.

## Patram

Postal Accounts Transaction Maintenance Software:

The PATRAM (Postal Accounts Transaction Maintenance) Software has been designed to maintain all accounting details currently being maintained in various registers. It emulates the auditing functions carried out by the Cash Certificates Section. The PATRAM software consists of 18 modules. This system was developed taking Tamil Nadu Postal Circle as the pilot site and replicated at other sites in the country subsequently.

## System for Civil Supplies and Consumer Protection Department

### *Family Card Maintenance System*

A workflow based Family Card Maintenance System has been developed for the Department of Civil Supplies and Consumer Protection Department, to assist in maintenance of consumer database. Citizens interact with the AC/TSO offices for issue of new family cards, various types of alterations to existing cards, issue of surrender certificates, etc. The software provides a work flow application to manage these services at the AC/TSO offices. All the TSO and Assistant Commissioners' Offices, are provided with internet connectivity. The card database in the central server at the office of the Commissioner of Civil Supplies, is kept updated through online interaction with all the AC/TSO offices. This provides accurate data for computing card-wise entitlement, which is used for preparation of Shop-wise, Talukwise, and District-wise monthly allotment statements.

### *SIM Card Management System (BSNL)*

The SIM Card Management System is an intranet application designed - to handle sale transactions at Customer Support Centres; to carry out all activities related to SIM card/ GSM number distribution/ allotment by the headquarters; and to maintain accounts; through a centralised database. The SIM Card Management system uses intranet technology to give a cost-effective solution that delivers powerful and robust results. By connecting Customer Support Centres, dealers, and distributors with the Mobile Services headquarters, through a centralised server, information is managed effectively and efficiently.

### *Chennai Corporation*

Ten Zonal Offices of Corporation of Chennai make use of the intranet based systems developed for Property Tax collection, Birth/ Death Certificates extraction, Company Tax collection, etc by accessing the central server located at Head Office.

### *Text Books Online*

The entire text books of school children under School Education Department, Tamil Nadu Government is available online.

## Geographical Information System (GIS)

Web GIS tools under Open Source environment have been used for developing the TN Maps site http://tnmaps.tn.nic.in. The tools have also been used for generating dynamic maps using Census 2001 data at http://www.census.tn.nic.in.

## e-Filing of Returns by Dealers for Department of Commercial Taxes

All the dealers in Tamil Nadu are filing their VAT monthly returns online through the website.

## Digital Certificates

PKI enabled application systems were developed for Madras Export Processing Special Economic Zone (MEPZ SEZ) to facilitate exporters registered with the Zone to file their Applications and Quarterly/Annual Returns through the Internet.

## Web Services

The website of Government of Tamil Nadu is being maintained by NIC and has large number of citizen oriented particulars such as Policy Notes of all the departments, Citizen Charter, RTI documents, Government Orders of Public Interest, Public Utility Forms, Tender Notices, Press Releases, Contact details, Statistical Reports, Acts and Rules documents, etc. The websites of all the districts and those of many departments have been developed and hosted by NIC. The GPF particulars of more than 5 lakh employees of the State are hosted on the web through the website of Accountant General of Tamil Nadu. Pension processing status is also made available through the website.

Online Registration System is used for the examinations conducted by the Tamil Nadu Public Service Commission. More than twenty thousand applications have been received online in the last two years for various examinations.

## Electoral data

All the 234 Assembly Constituencies are hosted on the web with interface to search the data in Tamil.

## Examination Results

The examination results of the Teachers Recruitment Board are hosted on the web. Tenth and Twelfth Standard examination results were accessed by more than 20 lakh users are hosted every year from 1997 (one of the first States to have exam results online). E-Governance is a continuous journey and Tamil Nadu has been an active State in this mission mode journey.

# 6

# e-Governance in Tamil for Tamil Virtual University

— G. Amirtharaj, Dr. A. James and
Dr. P.R. Nakkeeran

**ABSTRACT**

*Information and Communication Technology (ICT) has today become an integral part of governance, especially in India. ICT is viewed as a tool that will help deliver services in both public and private sector faster and transparent to end users. e-Governance, as a concept, involves leveraging ICT to streamline the administrative process. It involves computerization of records, facilitating efficient transactions between various departments using web portals and other electronic data transfer mechanisms to bring administration more effectively, to achieve the goals faster and ease.*

*Around the world various private, public and Government sectors are implementing the e-Governance to make their process transparent, cost effective, providing any where any time access of services and to reduce the processing time of their work flows. In order to make the process transparent, cost effective and to reduce the processing time Tamil Virtual University Management has decided to implement the e-Governance in Tamil Language for various activities like Employee Management, Time Management, Leave Management, Vendor Management, Work flow management, Course management, stock management etc...*

## Introduction

This chapter speaks about the implementation of e-Governance web based application in Tamil language for TVU with the Tamil Unicode support. Tamil Virtual University (www.tamilvu.org) is a Tamil Nadu Government Organization aims at providing Internet based resources and opportunities for the Tamil communities living in different parts of the globe as well as others interested in learning Tamil and acquiring knowledge of the history, art, literature and culture of the Tamils. The functions of TVU include Internet based Educational Programs, Digital Library and Development of Tamil computing.

As part of e-Governance initiative, the TVU management embarked on a paper-less office drive for introducing transparency and accountability in its internal and external transactions with vendors. As an initiative TVU has started developing a web based platform independent e-Governance tool using Java, Struts Framework and MYSQL database with Tamil Unicode support.

## Towards Implementation of e-Governance Applications for TVU

This e-Governance application is a web based application developed using Java Technologies (JSP and Servlets) and Struts Framework, MYSQL database as backend, Apache web server and Tomcat application server running in Linux OS with Tamil Unicode Support. The backend database is developed using MYSQL. It is configured to store Tamil

Unicode Characters. This application allows to key in Tamil and English characters by toggle between English and Tamil language. The data transactions between client and server are secured by Secured Socket Layer (SSL) enabled Apache web server.

## Application Architecture

The below diagram (Fig. 6.1) describes the architecture of the e-governance application for TVU.

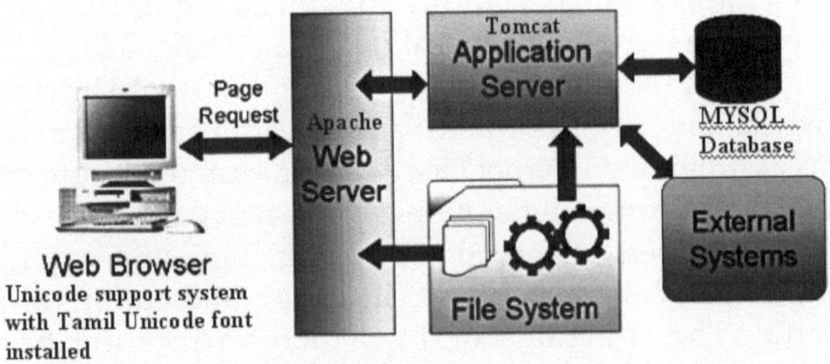


**Fig. 6.1 : Application Architecture**

Web Browser—Unicode (UTF-8) supported system with Tamil Unicode font installed to view the application pages by the end users. Apache web server—to serve the html, images and media content. Tomcat Application server—java container to run the JSP/Servlet. All the requests/response should be receive/sent in UTF-8 encoding format to support Tamil Unicode encoding scheme. MYSQL database—UTF-8 supporting database tables to store Tamil Unicode characters. File System—Configuration Management System to store electronic forms of documents/files. External System—Online Payment System (Currently ICICI payment gateway).

Now we will look into the details of each application:

## Gateway Portal

This web portal is the gateway to access all the applications in a single window. Each entity i.e. employees, study centre admin, vendors and students will be created with unique user name and password through user management module. An authorized admin will give access to create/update the user details.

The user can login into this portal and access the different application modules based on their role. This portal can be accessed from anywhere at anytime through web browser with internet connection enabled and also through intranet.

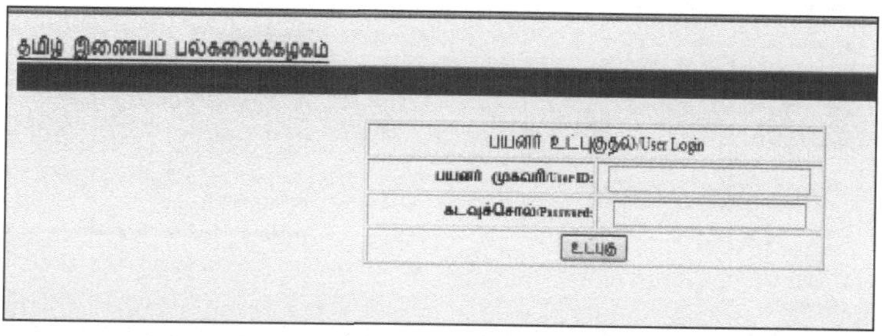


**Fig. 6.2 : Login Screen**

## Employee Management

This application is to manage the TVU employee details and Personal Registry (PR). Admin person can add new employee and update the user detail through the CRUD (Create Read Update Delete) process. A user (TVU staff) login into the e-Governance portal can view their details like their personal detail, skill detail, years of experience, designation and his manager hierarchy. The employee will be allowed to update his personal details only.

In TVU, personal registry was maintained by entering their daily activities manually in a physical notebook, routed to the reporting authority through attendant and verified. e-Governance facilitates online filing daily status, after implementing this module the employee will enter their work details in the online form and submit will intimate their immediate managers through mail to give their approval. The managers will login to the portal and view the pending PR's for approval. The manager can give their approval through a single mouse click after verifying the details. Here the employee can generate their work report of his/her own or his/her sub-ordinates. The reports can be generated monthly wise or a whole.

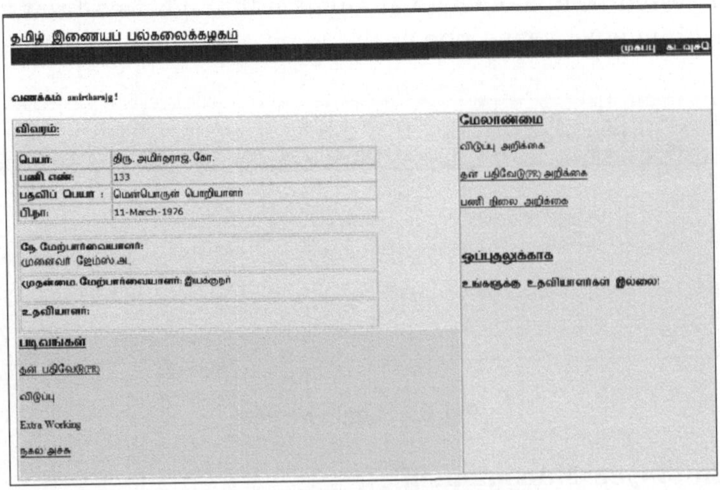


**Fig. 6.3 : Employee Home Page**

## Time Management

As part of the e-Governance, TVU has implemented the thumb impression attendance machine (Biometric system) from a third party. Until recently the TVU staff has to put their signature on the physical attendance book daily but it will not have the details of in-time or out-time.

For payroll calculation, a clerical person has to verify manually for each month and based on that monthly salary will be calculated. After implementing the Bio-metric thumb impression attendance machine now the employee has to give his/her thumb impression while entering or leaving the main entrance every time. The data will be collected in SQL server database with all the in-time and outtime details. A standalone reporting tool has been provided to generate/view the reports.

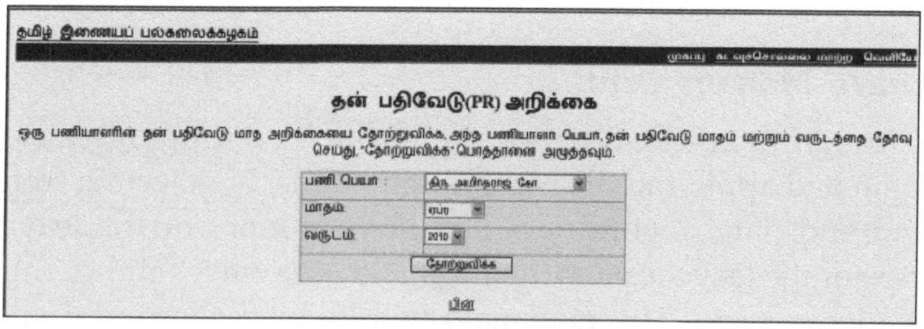


Fig. 6.4. PR Report

Every two weeks reports will be generated and sent to all the employees through mail. In the near future, the SQL server database will be integrated with our e-Governance portal so that each employee can generate their reports of

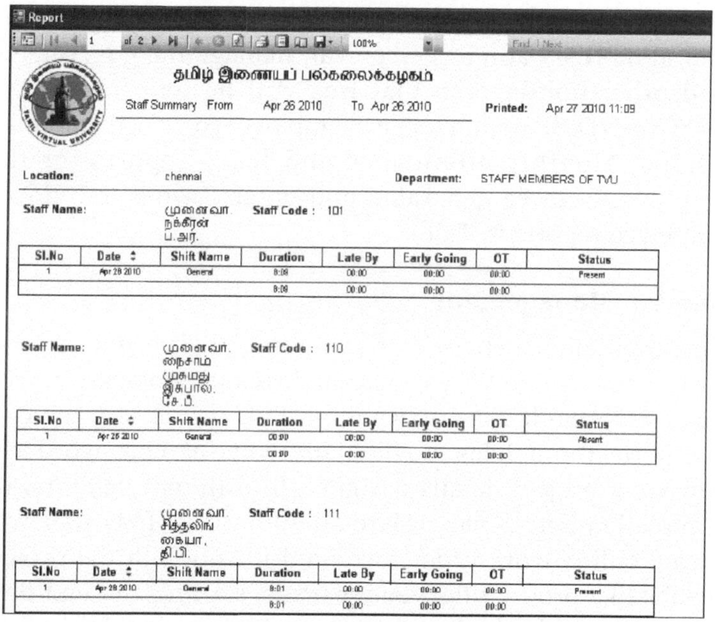


Fig. 6.5 : Attendance Report

their own or for their sub-ordinates and can view through the portal itself. And also the accounts department can get the consolidated month wise report of all the employees.

### Leave Management

Through the e-Governance portal the TVU employees can login and apply their leave through online, by selecting from and end date (including a half day), reason for the leave, type of the leave (casual, medical and earn leave) and submit the leave form. The managers will login to the portal and view the pending leave forms for approval. The manager can give their approval through a single mouse click.

The employee can apply/approve the leave from anywhere at anytime. This application will be integrated with the Bio-metric attendance machine database so that if an employee forgot to apply leave forms will automatically assigned leave for that particular day. Through this application and authorized admin person can manage the government and other holidays so that this will be reflected in the 'MYCLANDER' option for each employee to view the holiday details. Monthly attendance and leave reports for the employees can be generated and other various individual employee reports in Tamil.

### Vendor Management

This application is envisage to mange the TVU vendors, project details assigned to the various vendors and quotation/tender details. Through this application a TVU vendor can login to this portal through his provided username and password and can view project details assigned to different vendors, its completion details etc... Here an authorized TVU staff will create online work order form and fill up with the project details like project title, vendor name, starting and end date of a project and submit will go for the approval to the concern approval authority, once it has been approved a final output will be taken with the authorized signature and provided to the vendor. The approval authority will assign a particular project to a TVU employee to follow-up the project. Now that employee and his sub-ordinate will get the full details of the project in the e-governance portal though his login. The employee can track the project and follow up the vendor until the project completes. All the communication, demos, project status, vendor visiting detail, CD's submission etc... will be stored corresponding to this project and the higher authorities can the view the details at anytime. A detail report of project details and status of the project can be generated based on different criteria like project wise, vendor wise etc...

### Work Flow Management

Through this application the TVU staff members can submit the online Xerox/Print. Only after approval form authorities regarding details like number of copies and etc...actual printing takes place. The admin will take the Print/Xerox and update the form with actual number of copies taken and submit will go the supervisor for approval. The admin can generate the Xerox/print taken reports based on different criteria like for a particular month, by an employee, on particular device etc...

### Course Management

This application is to manage TVU Study centre across the globe, student, providing permission to access the online examination for a students, generating question papers for online and offline examinations, conducting or monitoring of online examination, mark sheet and certificate generation for students and examination result publishing. The study admin can login to the portal and allowed to register a new student for a course, to pay students course fee, register for a examination, providing permission for offline and online examination for their students, password reset etc...

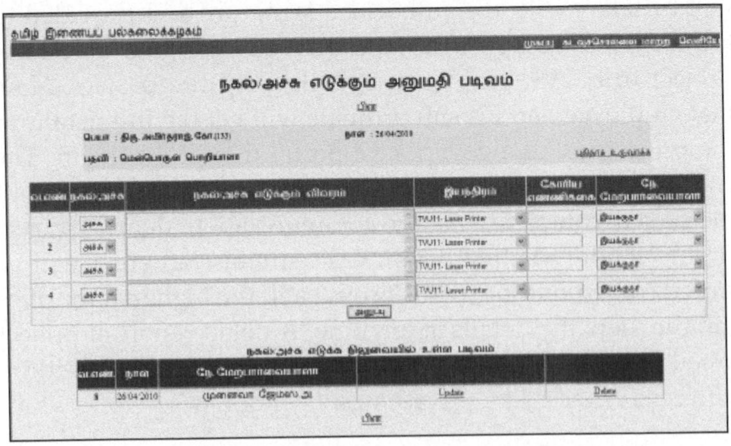

**Fig. 6.6. Xerox/Print Request Form**

TVU student registered for a course will be provided with unique username and password and the student can access the portal to view the examination schedule, online examination samples, question pattern samples for both online and offline examinations, exam results and mark sheet. TVU examination controller or the authorized TVU employee can register a new student for courses, register a student for examination, password reset, publishing examination results, generating examination report and sent to the study centre.

## Physical Stock Management

Now in TVU assets like furniture, computers hardware and software, Physical library books and course materials, Course CD's, Electrical accessories, paper and other office accessories are maintained in the physical register. The existing stock management is very cumbersome and difficult to integrate purchasing of available stock with consumables.

Through this e-Governance portal an interface will be provided to the authorized TVU staff to add new asset through the online form in different category like furniture, electrical, computer etc..., of type consumable and non-consumable and with other details like date of purchase, make, vendor and support/service contact details, warranty and location details. After submitting the online form an asset ID will be generated. Then the higher authority will verify and give his approval. The new items will be tagged with the generated asset ID. If a non consumable is abandoned or consumable has been used, through this application interface the details will be updated for that particular asset and submit. And this application will allow authorized TVU staff to generate the report based on various criteria.

## Conclusion

This chapter has discussed about the implementation of e-Governance web based portal in Tamil language for TVU with the Tamil Unicode support. By implementing the e-Governance application in localized Tamil language using Tamil Unicode encoding scheme, it will remove the language barriers in implementing e-Governance application in all the Government departments to facilitate efficient transactions between various departments and public using web portals and other electronic data transfer mechanisms through single window to bring administration more effectively, paper-less office drive and to provide effective services to the public.

# 7

# e-Resources are the Best Information Service to Teach, Learn and Research Through World Wide Web

*— V. Thangavel*

**ABSTRACT**

*The chapter highlights the usage trends of access to e-Resources in Indian Universities, Colleges and Research centre. The preliminary findings proceedings abstract of various conference of last ten years revealed that there is an upward trend. The paper briefly describes open access e-Resources used by the various scholars through World Wide Web in India: A citation Analysis Key Words: e-Resources, Consortiums, Information Sharing, e-Books, e-Journals, e-Magazine, e-Thesis, e-paper, e-Library, e-Publishing, Digital or Virtual Library, e-Lifestyle, e-Government, e-Directories.*

## Introduction

World wide web has created a sea change in providing information and as well as information transfer, Information scientists have undergone a perceptible change and have become IT centered, which is evinced from the publications pattern of articles, citations in journals, seminars, conferences ect., The world wide web provides access to materials that were previously not available to the researchers, students and faculty now able to view, listen to, and read materials that just few years ago were difficult, if not impossible, to access. Images, texts, historical documents, video clips, sound files etc, are now available over the web to anyone that has internet access. Almost any one can put almost anything online, and because that information is not filtered or mediated in any way. Academic, Research and development organizations are supported by well equipped library and information services unit to augment the objectives of the parent organizations. Proliferation of knowledge growth has resulted in information explosion, which has made the users so difficult to find the relevant information of research and development.

The modern libraries are able to provide information services to their patrons more efficiently with applications of information communication technology (ICT) in their environment, which satisfy the currency of information. In the recent years, the publishers and the professional societies are able to add value to their publications by means of providing the full text contents in electronic form. The networked environment of the organizations and the availability of internet connectivity give the users and easy access to the full text of the document.

## Purpose

The purpose of present chapter is to determine the awareness of electronic resources among library users and promote the usage of electronic resources by the students and members of faculty in engineering colleges in Tamil Nadu. Questionnaire was distributed to 210 randomly selected faculty and students in the various research institutions in Tamil Nadu. The researcher collected many articles i.e. print and online.

Nearly 54 articles have been received. Through this articles we identified the use of e-resources for various purpose i.e. teach, learn and research. Majority o the user using for research purpose. The 40% of user using for teaching purpose. The considerable percentage of users is using the e-resources for learning purpose. Through this articles reveals that the researcher and faculties are using e-resources through www, so the user's categories also increase day by day. Because the Government also to allot more fund innovative consortium for the user categories. In future e-resources are a pillar for servicing various information.

## Retrieval Systems

The study is an attempt to determine the level of using various types of resources by the research scholar in various University, Scholars felt that about various issue surrounding the electronic resources and whether changing attitude depend upon subject. Further reports have been presented about the factors supporting the growth and academic work with the help of web. The world of academics enjoying the fruits of electronic resources by the way of resources retrieval is highly thankful to the person like Tim Bern Lee for their tremendous effort. The 50 per cent web resources as noted by the respondents give the positive signs of the growth of IT world in the academic venture. Though the users of the web are having basic knowledge to handle the electronic resources, the institution involved in academic work should provide technical training to their students. The free internet access available in most of the universities may be retained and may be extended to other universities also. The mushrooming of new website development may lead to unreliable resources to the students at large and the research scholars in particular, hence, a board may be constituted to check the validity of resources before it is uploaded in to the web.

## e-Resources

*e-Publishing*: Electronic publishing (e-publishing) is 16 years old and the first e-book was published in Germany in 1985. The products of e-Publishing are mostly secondary sources, reference materials and the primary periodicals. The problems associated with e-Publications are integration with traditional forms, cost of acquisition, collection development, non-availability of selection tools, etc. These challenges should be taken as opportunities and prepared to find out the standards. When the father of the printing press, John Gutenberg, looked towards the future, he could never have dreamed that one small invention could revolutionize the world. The gift of publishing benefited not only the authors who could now create new words, but also the readers who would be exposed to new ideas, and new concepts. The creation of the printing press sparked a new revolution-a literary revolution. Now, with the widespread availability of computers and the internet, technology, enables virtually anyone to self-publish their literary works. e-Publishing is primed to revolutionize the world, by giving every individual the ability to publish their ideas, stories, books, without the prohibitive costs associated with conventional publishing. E-publishing is a process for production of typeset-quality documents containing text, graphics, pictures, tables, equations etc. In general, it is used to mean any information source published in electronic

## e-Books

Libraries form a vital part of the world's systems of education and information storage and retrieval. They make available—through books, films, recordings, and other media-knowledge that has been accumulated through the ages. People in all walks of like-including students, teachers, business executives, government officials, scholars and scientists—use library resources in their work. Large numbers of people also turn to libraries to satisfy a desire for knowledge or to obtain material for some kind of leisure-time activity. In addition, many people enjoy book discussions, film shows, lectures, and other activities that are provided by their local library. There are a considerable number of concepts being explored in future libraries research and development. The focus is in distributed and local collections of information objects - in the hybrid library including analogue as well as digital objects and on ways of identifying objects of interest to a user and arranging for the user to access them. The library of the future will be less a place where information is kept than a portal through which students and faculty will access the vast information resources of the world. The library of the future will be about access and knowledge management, not about ownership.

## e-Journals

Advancement in science and technology has changed the knowledge communication in the form of emedia. Order of the day is e-publishing and tradition print sources are replaced by e-sources. An attempt has been made to study the utilization and satisfaction among the users of various institutions and research centers towards e-journals using survey. The modern society is dynamic and complex. The duty of the research scholar towards social change, scientific development and social uplift is undisputable. EJournals will definitely make its own impact on the users in terms of scholarly communication of research.

The change in information technology and digital library has made us to move from print to electronic media in terms of acquiring information resources and to provide services. Libraries are undergoing rapid changes due to the developments in information communication technology paper based resources are giving way to electronic resources. The CD ROM and E-journals are providing information to the user from various research communities. An attempt has been made in this study to identify the usage of CD ROMs and e-Resources among the various research communities in Tamil Nadu.

## e-Government

The term "e-Government" is used in this paper to denote the concept of using information communication Technology (ICT) as a means to organize and manage the administrative processes of the government, especially the interactive processes between the government and the public. Though ICT has been available widely for more than four decades and many governments around the world have indeed used ICT in certain aspect of government, the concept of e-Government is relatively new in the sense mentioned above. Only a handful of governments have progressed to a high degree in harnessing the immense power of ICT in re-organizing their government infrastructure and in serving their citizenry, and have done so in an efficient and effective manner. e-Government is not mere 'technologising' of government. It is not just a matter of automating some manual processes nor is it a simple introduction of technology where none existed. e-Government requires a fundamental re-thinking of governance itself and, as some have suggested, re-inventing of government. If bureaucracy is the invention of the 19th century, we might say e-Government is the invention of the 21st century. e-Government re-examines the organizing principles of bureaucracy and governance, re-defines the objectives and deliverables of government and re-deploys the resources available. In this process of re-invention, the basic intent is both refinement of the old and introduction of the new. e-Government is NOT throwing the baby with the bathwater.

## Consortiums for e-Resources

Consortium a strategic alliance of libraries with a common interest, not under the same institutional control, but usually restricted to a geographical area, number of libraries, types of materials, or subject of interest, which is established to develop and implement resource sharing among member. This chapter discussed about the benefits and limitations of e-Resources through consortium. Makes a comparative study of two major library consortium of India i.e. INDEST-AICTE and UGC-INFONET in terms of objectives, governance, members, access pattern, resources etc. Analysis the study and makes suitable suggestions for its improvement. Concludes with the remarks that these consortiums will bring remarkable change in the library scenario and also the educational system of India. In modern library environment, information technology is playing a pivotal role. Today's technology, interactivity, digital media, expanding network and communications capabilities compel the libraries to move from organizational self-sufficiency to a collaborative mode of acquisition of library materials. Library consortia are one of the emerging tool kits. The consortium should take a lead role in the development of a national strategy for information provision for research in higher education. Librarians should seriously rethink and reinitiate consortium movement like developed countries for maximum utilization of resources at a reduced cost, time and space. It is an encouraging sign that both INDEST-AICET and UGC INFONET consortia are functioning well. These will bring remarkable change in the library scenario as well as the educational system of India.

The UGC-INFONET programme will be a boon to higher education systems in several ways. It is a vehicle for distance learning to facilitate the quality education all over the country. It is a major source for research scholars for tapping the most up-to-date information. It is a medium for collaboration among research guide and research scholars. One of the major developments in libraries and information systems in the past 15 years is the advent and spread of electronic information resources, services and networks mainly as a result of developments in information and communication technologies. The change is basically of physical form where information content is increasingly being captured, processed, stored and disseminated in electronic form. The unique features of the information needs of users in electronic environments relate to the physical form in which information content is made available in electronic information environments. Users normally desire the content to be made available within the constraints of their skills and technological capabilities so that it is possible to access and use the required information content to resolve the felt gap in knowledge.

The e-Journal programme is corner stone of the UGC-Infonet effort which aims at addressing the teaching, learning and research collectively and governance requirements of the universities and research centers. It would facilitate free access to scholarly journals and databases in all areas of learning to the research and academic community. This articles discusses the need for sharing of electronic resources among Libraries and Information Centers in developing countries. Highlights the importance of 'Library consortia' in this digital era, stating its salient features, functions and responsibilities. Examines in detail the emergence of various resource sharing models in the developing countries with special reference to India.

## Emergence of Library Networks in India

In India library networks actually started due to the initiatives by NISSAT in forming CALIBNET in 1986, DELNET in 1988 and another networks subsequently. The UGC (University Grants Commission, India) set up INFLIBNET in 1988, NIC (National Informatics Centre) also set up DELNET, which are the first operational library networks in India. CALIBENT and INFLIBNET have not been able to project their performance as they were planned but they are trying to achieve their goal. Functions, organizations, cooperation's, progress and creation of databases amongst libraries of BONET and CALIBNET as library networks are still dissatisfactory. Institute of Economic Growth (IEG) was founded in 1958 as a autonomous institution recognized by the University of Delhi. The IEG library has its networking with different libraries e.g. Ratan Tata Library, Delhi School of Economics, Delhi University library. NCAER library, IIPA Library, DELNET etc. for helping the readers in getting the desired books and journals which are not available in the IEG library on inter-library loan basis. There are other examples of networking and resource sharing of Astronomy libraries in India. They jointly established a networking for resource sharing amongst the libraries e.g. Indian Institute of Astrophysics (IIA) library, Inter- University Centre for Astronomy and Astrophysics (IUCAA) Library, National Centre for Astronomy and Astrophysics (NCRA) Library, Nizamiah Observatory (NO) Library, Physical Research Laboratory (PRL) Library, Raman Research Institute (RBI) Library, Tata Institute of Fundamental Research (FIFR) Library, Uttar Pradesh State Observatory (UPSO) Library. The main purposes of this networking are for better resource sharing, to reduce costs, for speedy delivery of documents, to keep abreast of new developments etc. No efforts have been made in India to network public libraries though it is very much essential to cater networked information to the general public where more than 70 per cent of the total people are residing in rural areas. However, much emphasis should be given at the national level in India for the development of documentary information resources because it is considered as one of the vital resources to promote the development of economy, science, technology and culture etc.

## Resource Sharing Networking Models

The fundamental object of information resource sharing is to solve the problems faced by the libraries such as information explosion, several needs of users, increasing cost of subscribing periodicals, sharing library budgets, fluctuation of the exchange rates etc. Now-a-days, to solve the above problems different resource sharing networking models are observed at local, regional, national and international levels. Generally, there are three levels of national resource sharing networks exist:

(a) ***Local:*** Information is stored in local libraries in the form of Union Catalog for local collection available in local libraries:

(b) ***Regional:*** Information is stored in regional libraries and services are provided on broad subject area basis; and

(c) ***National:*** Information is stored in national library in the form of national Union Catalog for normally national collection available in national library and services are rendered to users as national resources. There are four existing resource sharing networking models, which have been shown in tabular form in Table.

**Table 7.1 : Various Models to Resource Sharing**

| Model | Aims & Funding | Examples |
|---|---|---|
| Centralized collection development and services at national and regional level | *Resources*: Acquired centrally and stored at single site<br>*Funding*: Contribution by participting libraries. Grants are also sought from government nd private agencies. | National Lending Library, UK. |
| Centralized collection development and services by subject | *Resources*: Subject specific collection of documentary resources. Acquired centrally and stored at a single site city, region or country may limit the geographic distribution of libraries.<br>*Funding*: Marketing of services and grants from the government and private agencies. | National Service Library at INSDOC, New Delhi |
| Centralized collection development at organizational level | *Resouces*: Libraries belonging to a single bigger organization collaborate. The shared collection is acquired centrally at a single site.<br>*Funding*: Organization backing the library provide funds. The participating libraries may also contribute towards the central funds. | CSIR, DRDO, DOE, ISRO |
| Coordinated collection development at institutional level | *Resources*: Eliminates duplications. Serves at the level of participating libraries. The geographical area of cooperation could confine to a city, region or country.<br>*Funding*: The individual libraries determine their level of support. User libraries pay for the services they avail of. | Delnet, Bonet, Malibent |

UGC—Infonet Electronic Journal Consortium is an innovative project launched by University Grant Commission (UGC) to promote the use of electronic data bases and full text access to journals by the research and academic community in the country. This project will bring about a qualitative change in the academic environment. The research and academic environment. The research and academic community can now have an access to resources at their finger tips.

## Consortia Initiatives in India

The information revolution and proliferation have brought about drastic changes to the function and service in all types of libraries in India during last two decades. Many libraries in India till today are not in affording position to procure all documents and subscribe to core journals in major disciplines or CDROM databases, due to their financial crunch. At the national level, the UGC (University Grant Commission, India) setup INFLIBENT in 1988. It has taken imitation about a formidable change in developing adequate infrastructure in libraries, especially university libraries, to be a part in the networked environment. Since January 2004, University Grants Commission through its one point programme (UGC) / INFONET is providing access to e-subscription to all-important journals for the entire university community. The Ministry of Human Resource Development (MHRD) through its INDEST (Indian National Digital Library in Science and Technology) has launched consortia-based subscription to electronic resources for higher - technical education systems in India.

Besides, there are a few national and regional library consortia developed in the recent years. Council of Scientific and Industrial Research (CSIR) Tata Institute of Fundamental Research (TIFR), Department of Atomic Energy (DAE), Indian Institute of Technology (IIT), and Indian Institute of Management (IIM) have already formed their sectoral consortia and have been subscribing to electronic sources like Science Direct, MathSciNet, and Blackwell, John Wiley, ABI/INFORM and Business Sources Premier. Also, both Institute of Mathematical Science (IMSc) and TIFR have been subscribing to MathSciNet database under their own consortia consisting group of libraries in their region. And many more are expected to come soon.

Increasing the Discovery and use of e-Resources in University Libraries and Research Centres: There is a large quantity of subscribed e-Resources in our libraries and they contain quality information, though expensive. In spite of advantages in terms of access and search capabilities, they are underused. Systematic plan has to be in place for their promotion of use. While a good ICT infrastructure is a prerequisite, it alone will not do. Proactive strategies are required and these need to be adopted imaginatively. Access to e-Resources need to be made easier for both on campus and off campus users. As a priority, active users need to be identified and they need to be converted to heavy users of e-Resources.

Secondly, non-users be converted to active users Various methods have to be tried in order to grab the attention of the users towards the e-Resources. User training will increase the confidence level of the users. Traditional awareness methods include: Personal visits, user training, brochures, posters and displays. Newer technologies from the Web 2.0 such as RSS alert service, Blogs, Wikis and Facebook make the interaction with the library not only interesting but also add more value. Finally, the effectiveness of various promotional strategies need to be measured by monitoring the usage and user feed back.This research sought to determine use of online resources and databases and to assess current user characteristics associated with use of online resources by the Faculty and researcher of various universities.

## Suggestions

1. The university library should make necessary arrangement for continuing subscription for the on line journals along with print journals.
2. The University library should conduct orientation, training programme regularly to assist the users of agricultural consortium programme.
3. The authorities of the university should take keen interest for providing better infrastructure facilities for the improvement of Internet speed, e-Journals, e-Books, e-Directories, e-Conference proceedings, ethesis, e-Dissertation and e-Dictionaries. So that users can feel more comfortable in browsing on line information.

## Conclusion

Remote access of e-Resources has been a major boon to academic and research libraries. Online journals are considered the note chord of any library's collection and have become indispensable for research in any field. Many online journals available in the form of databases as well as they directly access through the Internet. The quantity of online journals is growing larger and has become a quite visible entity in serial publication. Today most of the online journals appear as parallel version of its print counterparts and more publishers are making their journals available in electronic format. Many academic institutions are currently building substantial collections of full-text journals and continue to increase access to various online databases. Because these resources come at a great cost, it becomes important to understand database and full-text journal use among university patrons and the characteristics accompanying today's remote and in-house library users. Increased access to computers, the Internet, online databases full text journals necessitates reassessing online use patterns and user characteristics.

Nowadays it is impossible for libraries to procure all the documents and subscribe to core journals that are in demand by the users. There are many online journals and databases are available open access. Subscription of online journals and databases through the consortium(s) are much economic for the libraries.

## REFERENCES


1. ISI Reseachsoft.2003a.*EndNote-Product Information*, 5 August 2002,
2. Asksamsystems.2003, cittion *Bibliographic and Research Note Software*, 15 February 2003,
3. Craztsqyurrek cinoekte siytuibs, 2003 Refas—*The Reference Assistant*, 2002,
4. Scholars aid inc.2003 is Scholars Aid Right for You?, 27 August 2002, http://scholarsid.com/ right4 you_research.html
5. Brown, C.M. 1999, "Information Seeking Behaviour of Scientists in the Electronic Information Age: Astronomers, Chemists, Mathematicians, and Physicists: *Journals of the American society for Inforamtion Sceince* 50 (10): pp 929-943.
6. Green, R (2000) Locating Sources in Humanities Scholarship: The Efficacy of Following Bibliographic References, *Library quarterly* 70 (2) pp 201-229.
7. Bates, M J (2002) The Cascade of Interactions in the Digital Interface. *Information Processing and Management*, 38 (3), 381-400.
8. MathesA (2005) *Preserving Public Domain Books.*
9. Barrett A (2005) The Information Seeking Habits of Graduate Student Researchers in the Humanities. *The Journal of Academic Librarianship*, 31(4), pp.324-331.
10. Workloc, Kate (2002) Electronic Journals: User Realities—*The Trusty About Content Usage Among the STM Community*, Learned Publishing 15 (3): pp.223-226.

# 8

# Use of e-Resources by the Research Scholars and Faculty of Management Studies in Management Research Centres, Tamil Nadu

—V. Thangavel and Dr. V. Ramesh

**ABSTRACT**

*The electronic resources have the effect of democratizing the research community. The study is an attempt to determine the level of using various types of resources by the research scholar. Research scholars felt that the electronic resources would be useful to carry out their research and do their further research works, depending on their subject. This chapter discusses about the use of electronic resources by the research scholars and faculties of management studies through World Wide Web in Chennai, Tamil Nadu.*

## Introduction

Computer-based automation was initially incorporated into library operations as a mechanism for handling the routine functions of running a library such as circulation, cataloging, acquisitions, interlibrary loan and serials control. Systems for handling these operations became available able to the larger library community from the early 1970s onward, although there were some earlier pioneers with well developed local systems. Early systems were typically run on large computers into which data were entered, processed behind the scenes, and returned as printed output of some type (overdue notices, invoices, or catalog cards, for example). Pioneers in reference database services, such as DIALG, also operated using large mainframe computers to which patrons connected via terminals and required experienced searchers mastering a complex set of commands to generate effective search results.

The modern society is dynamic and complex. The duty of research scholar should know the availability of sources in their topics. Electronic resources are available in various formats. The different types of electronic resources are electronic books, electronic journals, electronic databases, search engines and subject gateways.

## Public Services

Electronic resources are changing the longstanding relationship which traditionally existed between library professionals and users. Formerly, the use of resources and services required patrons to visit the library. Print indexes in the reference area provided needed citations the card catalog indicated whether that library owned a particular item, and the circulation desk could place a hold for an item checked out to another patron. Early electronic tools such as DIALOG were available only to librarians who frequently consulted with users to refine their needs before conducting expensive and sometimes complex database searches. The introduction of large scale automated union catalogs like OCLC heave helped to revolutionize services such as interlibrary loan and library functions such as acquisitions and cataloging. The introductions of newer electronic resources have shifted services and functions from those which are librarian mediated to those specifically geared towards the end user. Advances such as the availability of online citation and document delivery services remotely accessed from a home or voice, 24 hour remote availability to OPACs providing both an item's current circulation status and the ability to place holds oneself, plus the increasing number of resources available directly to patrons through networks, have combined to eliminate the need for a visit to the reference desk, or the library in many cases, to satisfy information needs.

## Objectives

The following objectives are framed for study:

1. To evaluate the purpose of using electronic resources.
2. To identify the use of electronic resources.
3. To identify the purpose of electronic resources by the research scholars and faculty in various field in Management Research Centres, Chennai, Tamil Nadu.
4. To find out the best publicity method to promote the usage of electronic resources.
5. To identify the format of print or electronic resources and their performance.
6. To know the problems faced by Research Scholar in accessing electronic information.

## Literature Review

A good number of related studies on the usage of electronic resources have been conducted mainly in developing countries like India and developed countries. These studies led to know the status of the usage of the electronic resources against investment. Dugdale studied the library services at the Bolland Library, University of the west of England, Bristol in the UK and investigate the ways; in which students might be encouraged to use electronic resources and to develop important life long learning skills through the Reside (research, information, delivery) electronic library.

Ferguson stated that the university of Hong Kong in China had found that the change to a mostly electronic collection has been successful. He stated that 59 per cent patrons preferred reading electronics serials while 30 per cent favored the printed version. Only 14 per cent of the academic staff still favoured printed journals. Alwarammal R, Sivaraj S and Madasamy R stated that respondents were asked to mark their potential use of electronic journals by using a five-point scale of 0-4 where 0 indicated not satisfied and 4 meant highly satisfied. Assigned scores for each item were converted into mean scores. Frequency of responses for each resource and respective means scores are given.

It was found that Elsevier's science direct was the most used resource by the faculty and students in all engineering disciplines and it is receiving the highest means core of 2.32. It was followed by IEL online was the next used resource by the faculty and students of computer, electrical and electronics, electronics and communication and it is receiving the mean score of 1.91. It was followed by .51 and .64 mean score of ASCE and ASME resources used by civil and mechanical engineering students respectively. The other two resources of Nature and Nature biotechnology and management journals with a means score of .76 and .42 were mostly used by biotechnology and management students respectively.

## Methodology

The research scholars and faculties of various research organizations in Management Research Centers, Chennai, Tamil Nadu represented the target population for this study. The questionnaire method has been employed to collect the data for the present study. The questionnaire was constructed based on the following elements; use profile, frequency of visit, purpose of using online resources, acceptance of electronic media, awareness of the existence of electronic resources, publicity to promote the usage of electronic resources, paper presentation in conferences, papers published in Journals ( National and International ), publication details and reasons for non-use of electronic resources.

## Data Analysis

The data collected through questionnaires were organized and tabulated by using statistical methods and percentages. A total number of 450 questionnaires were randomly distributed among the faculty and researchers, out of which only 432 filled questionnaires were returned to the investigator. The response rate is 96 per cent.

## Sample

The population of this study is faculty and Research Scholars in Management studies in Management Research centres, Chennai, Tamil Nadu. The sample consists of 432 faculty members and Ph D students who filled in the questionnaire of the annual user survey of 2009-2010. Thus, the sample consists of self-selected volunteers and may be biased towards those who are most active users of electronic resources.

The analysis below indicates that the sample is reasonably representative by sex, discipline, occupation and university. However, some later findings hint that it is likely that active users of electronic resources are somewhat over-represented in the data. Inspection of the demographics of the respondents showed that the sample's breakdown by sex was nearly equivalent to the population. 50 per cent of university faculty and PhD students in Management Research Centers, Chennai, Tamil Nadu were women in 2009, whereas a in this study 50 per cent of the respondent were women.

## Suggestions

On the basis of the response and opinion given by the respondents some of the important suggestions have been made, which will help the effective use of the electronic resources.

1. The authorities of the university and research institutions should take keen interest for providing better infrastructure facilities for the improvement of internet speed, so that users can feel more comfortable in browsing e-Resources.
2. The university library and research institutions should make necessary arrangement for continuing subscription for the print journals along with e-Journals. Since more than 95 per cent of Research scholar are interested in making use of print journals.
3. The university library and research institutions should conduct orientation/training programmes regularly to assist the use of e-Resources.
4. Majority of the research scholar have suggested that UGC-INFONET and other library consortium and they should provide pdf files of science direct, wiley-interscience and all other scientific journals.

## Conclusion

One of the major developments in libraries and information systems in the past 10 years is the advent and spread of electronic resources, information services and networks mainly as a result of developments in information and communication technologies. The change is basically of physical form where information content is increasingly being captured, processed, stored and disseminated in electronic form. The unique features of the information needs of users in electronic environments relate to the physical form in which information content is made available in electronic information environments.

Users normally desire the content to be made available within the constraints of their skills and technological capabilities so that it is possible to access and use the required information content to resolve the felt gap in knowledge.

## REFERENCES


1. Ikhizama, B.O & Oruwole, A.A. (2003) Pttern of Usage of Inforamton Sources by Scientist in Nigerian Universities of Agriculture (UoA), *Library Progress*, 23 (1), pp. 1-6.
2. Julien, Heidi, & Michels, David (2000) Source Selection Among Information Seekers: Ideals and Realities, *Canadian Journal of Inforamation and Libray Science*, 25 (1), pp. 2-17.
3. Liu, Ziming (2006) , Print *vs.* Electroinc Resources: A Study of User Perceptions, preferences and Use, *Information Processing and Management*, 42 (2), 583-592.
4. K.P. Singh and M.P.Satija, (2007) Information Seeking Behaviour of Agricultural Scientists with Particular Reference to Their Information Seeking Strategies: *Annals of Library and information Studies*. Vol. 54, December 2007, pp.213-220.
5. M.Chandrashekara and K.R Mulla, (2007) The Usage Pattern of Electronic Information Resources Among the Engineering Research Community in Karnataka: A Survey. *Pearl Journal*; Vol.1, No. 4, October-December 2007. pp.33-38.
6. Alwarammal R, Sivaraj S and Madasamy R (2009), Promotion and Usage of Electronic Resources by the Students and Members of Faculty in Engineering Colleges in Tamil Nadu, India: *An Empirical Study*.
7. Knowledge Networking in ICT Era, *International Conference Proceedings*, Vol 2. pp.676-679.

# 9

# Quality Assessment Technique of e-Learning in Tamil Language

—A. Kovalan and Siva Pillai

**ABSTRACT**

*Web-based Teaching Learning Process (WBTLP) is a rapidly growing area in Education. Traditional forms of teacher education are transformed, as the Internet becomes a new medium for communication. Traditionally teachers have fulfilled dual roles as presenters of structured information and social agents in the educational process. Students are in need of good interactive resources with learning tools and techniques. Hence, there is a need for training in WBTLP so as to enable the teacher to provide good resources in the web. The web-based learner resources can improve the quality of teacher education by availing various tools and techniques of assessment. The assessment of web-based learning resources helps to provide quality web resources in teacher education. It is also used to help teacher to have better resources and environment in which teaching takes place.*

*The environment includes the organization, the learning materials, use of media, delivery methodology and various approaches in details.*

*Assessment is a judgement regarding the worth or value of something. Typically the assessment process is divided into two parts. The first is a teacher assessment, which relates to interaction and guidance of a teacher with students and the second is a learning resources assessment, which relates to quality of materials and resources of a course. However, the primary function of the assessment is to help teacher to improve the total quality of education in web teaching learning environment.*

## Introduction

The rise of e-Learning and web-based training in Teaching Learning Process in Tamil Language (TLPTL) has lead to a growth in the use of web-based learning assessment, which will increase as the use of e-Learning becomes more widespread. Designing web-based tools, making resources and quality assessment of the learning resources is a challenging task for educators, curriculum designers, computer programmer and evaluator of the resources in the Web-based Teaching Learning Process (WBTLP). The teacher in online should take special effort for implementation and development of the instructional resources which is clear, accessible support, simplicity, transparency of the educational materials, and likelihood of the students' misconceptions as a result of interacting with materials. The teacher or trainer assessment is also very important to learners' motivation, self-regulated learning, continues education, knowledge improvement, people with disability and poor social background. This paper presents an overview of web based learning assessment cycle in two different aspect viz. Web-based Learning Teacher Assessment Cycle (WBLTAC) and Web-based Learning Resources Assessment Cycle (WBLRAC).

## Web-based Learning Teacher Assessment Cycle

An online teacher/trainer plays a key role in developing and maintaining an effective online learning environment and possesses a unique set of skills to success of a student. A quality of online teacher is very important than any resources in online. The role of online teacher is not just respect their need; they need to be involved in proper guidance, formative and summative assessment, counseling, administration and learners' motivation. They should also support their feelings, and make facilitate to communicate with the learners with different media and methods. This means that the online teacher should make their time efficiently with their students. Hence, the quality of teacher/trainer can assess in six major categories viz.:

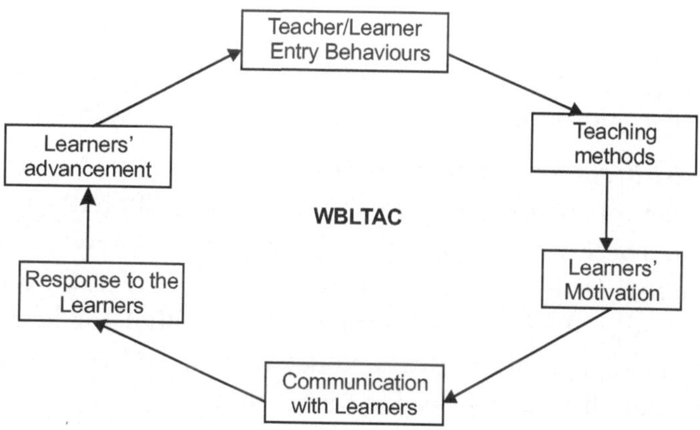


**Fig. 9.1 : Teaching Assessment Cycle (TAC)**

### *Teacher/Trainer Entry Behaviours*

Once you have identified a person as an online teacher/trainer for a specific task or target groups the organizer determine what kind of knowledge, skill, and experience need to be taken into account for the specific training process. The entry behaviour may be determined by three major areas viz.:

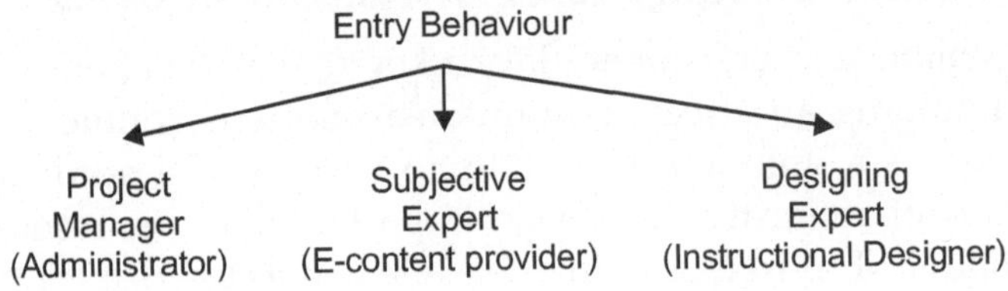


**Fig. 9.1.1 : Teacher Entry Behaviour**

***Project Manager :*** Project manager is an achievement of academic qualification, administrative power, attitude level, communicative ability, leadership quality, involvement in students' achievement, investigative technique of students' problems; task oriented training activities, cooperation with student on assignment, equal treatment made to each student, responsibility, freedom, and support by giving opportunity to express their opinion and relationship with students, teacher and designer.

***Subjective Expert:*** Subjective Expert is based on theoretical and experimental experience in a different content area. The e-Content provider should have knowledge of content development, material editing and method of teaching. e-Content development is essential for learner, multimedia producer, Instructional designer and distributors. These are the quality needed for bearing on the delivering of the training product/event.

***Designing Expert:*** Designing expert should have knowledge of expectation of an online learner. The e-Content material designer have different roles in a web based learning materials developing a project viz. instructional designer, multimedia designer, graphics artist, internet based application developer, media producer, and web administrator.

### *Teaching Methods*

Web-based trainer use different methods to deliver an instructional material. The structure of an online teaching method consists of following three components:

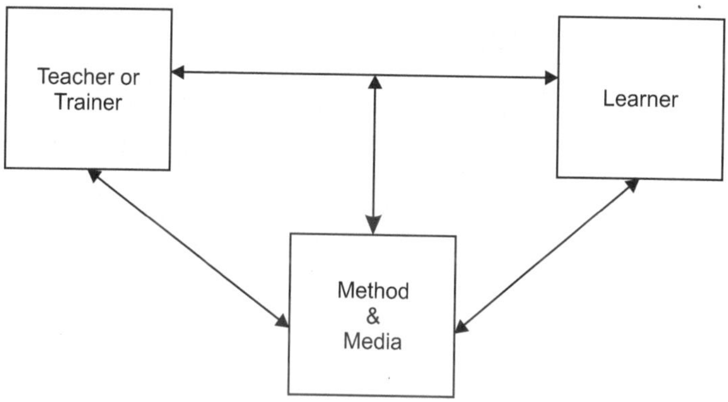


**Fig. 9.2. Structure of Teaching Method**

The trainer provides content in different media viz. text, pictures, audio, video, animation, and simulation which helps student to understand the concept easily. It implies that the learner has freedom to choose his choice by the way of his interest and preference of his learning materials.

### *Learners' Motivation*

Encourage learners to solve their problems by interaction with facilitator, peer group discussion, and expert in their chosen subject. The models of achievement motivation most often attribute students' academic motivation to cognitive processes (Bandura, 1986; Weiner, 1992) which regulate students' Teacher or Trainer Learner Method and Media learning behaviour. There is a growing body of evidence (Wentzel, 1991, 1994, 1996), however, that a consideration of social motivation of classrooms should not be excluded from the model of achievement motivation. Three aspect of learners' motivation is important in web-based teaching process viz.:

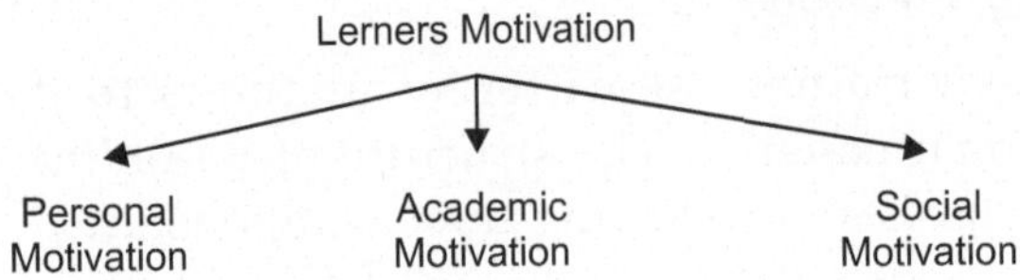


**Fig. 9.3 : Learners' Motivation**

Success at online teaching learning process requires students to achieve three outcomes of education: individual power, academic achievement, and social adjustment. Judgments on levels of motivation were made using the following criteria: teacher interaction with learners and individual pupils, time keeping, teaching style, and observed enthusiasm in different aspect.

## *Communication with Learner*

Continues communication with learner helps to overcome the isolation problems. Web based teacher have many channel to communicate with their learner viz.

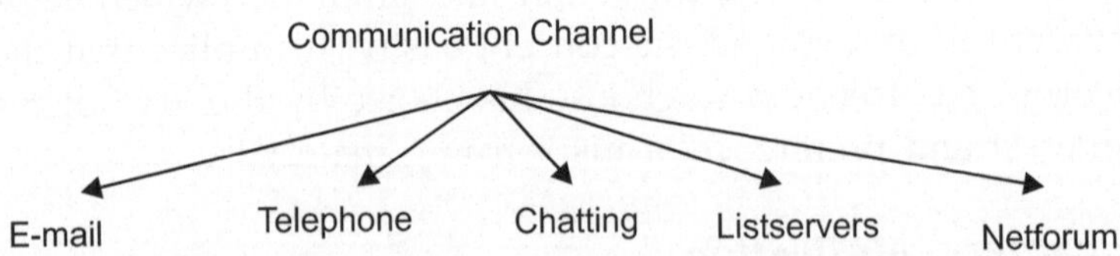


**Fig. 9.4. Learners' Communication Channel**

*Electronic mail (e-mail)* can be used by the facilitator and learners-to-learners communication. e-mail is cost-efficient, fast and convenient. Group e-mail can also be used to contact all learners simultaneously.

*The telephone* has used as a synchronous method of supporting the learners. The telephone allows learners to communicate with their teacher/trainer. Learners can discuss instructional and non-instructional problems with their facilitator.

**Chatting** helps to learner to communicate with his facilitator and his peer groups. Two types of chatting methods are available *viz.* video chatting and audio chatting. Video chatting is like a face-to-face communication and the audio chatting is like a telephone communication.

***List servers*** is an e-mail list that allows any of the users registered on the list to e-mail a specific list serve address, after which the e-mail is forwarded to everyone on the list. It is useful for the learner to discuss of topics relevant to the learning event.

**Net forum** allow the facilitator to post learning event information or announcements, changes to the learning event or deadlines for assignments. It is also used by learner to post questions about the learning event which the facilitator and other learner can answer. Learners and researchers are encouraged to discuss and reply in discussion forum.

## *Response to the Learner*

It is the quality of awareness that is evoked in collaborative meaning-making with students that defines the quality of a teacher's response to the teaching situation. Immediate feedback, which makes encourage, interest on further and continuing education, helps the learner to achieve their goal. A variety of possibilities exists. The teacher may have a word or phrase of affirmation:

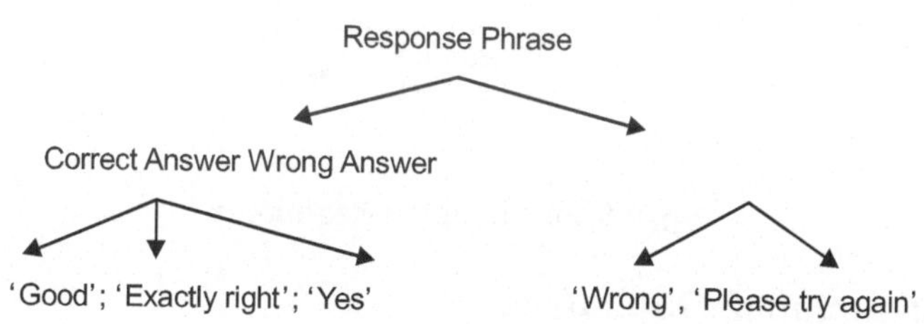


**Fig. 9.5. Teachers' Response Phrase**

### *Learners' Advancement*

Learners' record shows the quality of teacher/facilitator in web based teaching learning process. Ensuring the achievement of learners in different aspects *viz.* academic achievement, personal improvement, social behaviours, communication development, self-awareness, self-motivation, etc.

## Web-based Learning Resources Assessment Cycle

Instructional resources are plays an important role to deliver the learning materials through online. Using these resources, the learner can contact their facilitator at any time or in a fixed time when they are having problems. A quality resources make quality learning product and provide quality learner in web-based training process. The quality resources can be assessed by six major categorize viz.

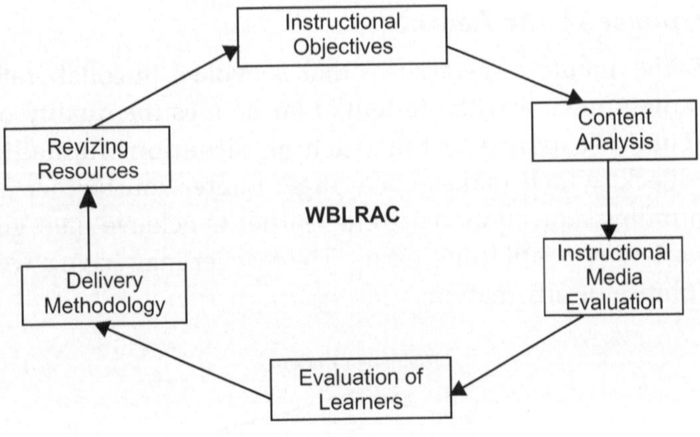


**Fig. 9.6. Instructional Resources**

### *Instructional Objectives*

Objectives are useful in content development, material designing and implementation of the web-based learning process and evaluation of the learner. The instructional objective describes a kind of performance expected by learners at the end of a learning event. The objective helps learner to plan the learning opportunity in their interested area. The development of instructional objectives is a task whose importance should not be overlooked. The instructional objectives can be divided into two major categories.

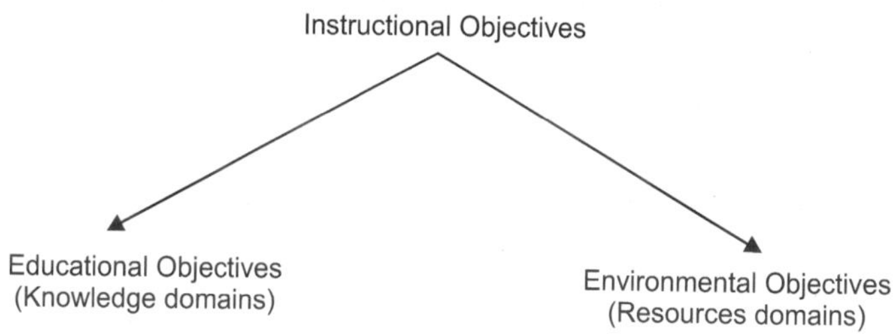


**Fig. 9.7. Learners' Instructional Objectives**

***Educational Objectives (EdO):*** Educational objectives help learners know where they are going and how they are going to achieve their goal. EdO is designed based on learners' interest and involvement. In this domain the facilitator investigate the learners' interest to achieve their goal.

***Environmental Objectives (EnO):*** This environment helps learner to achieve their goal at their own location. In virtual learning environment the learner gets freedom to choose their interest subject with establish guidelines for including graphics, videos, audios, animations, pictures, and various presentation media. This environment makes more benefits to a learner to achieve their goal without any strain and pain.

### Content Analysis

The content review team might include the client, instructional designer, subject-expert(s) and programmer. Developing new Learning Materials (LM) is a major task involving their design, development, delivery and evaluation to ensure their effectiveness. Check the existing materials before providing a new one. If there is large number of subject matter and other information relevant to the learners' achievement goal on the web, then it is probably suitable for web-based delivery. The LM should provide more opportunity to the learner to choose their specific content area. The learning event needs to be updated regularly. In content analysis the following points need to consider for analyzing to provide a better learning materials.

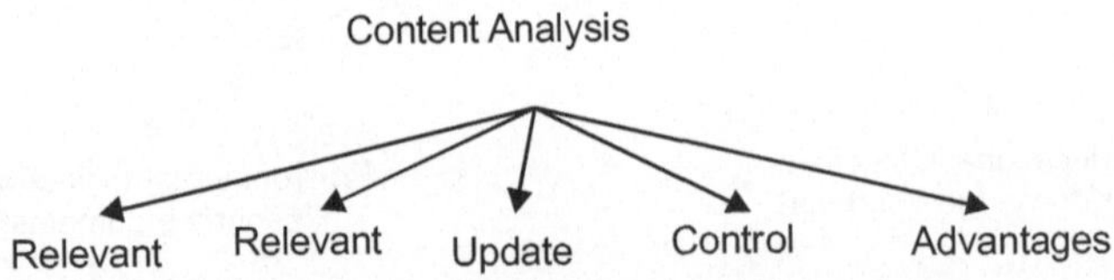


**Fig. 9.8. Learners' Content Analysis**

Analyze, how well the content and material presented in the way that was both interesting and stimulating. The evaluation of these materials should include gathering data regarding the relevance of various assignments and the quality of the various assessments.

### *Instructional Media Evaluation*

In an online environment, media are used to provide variety to what is essentially a text-based methodology. Such media may include video, although this is limited unless learners

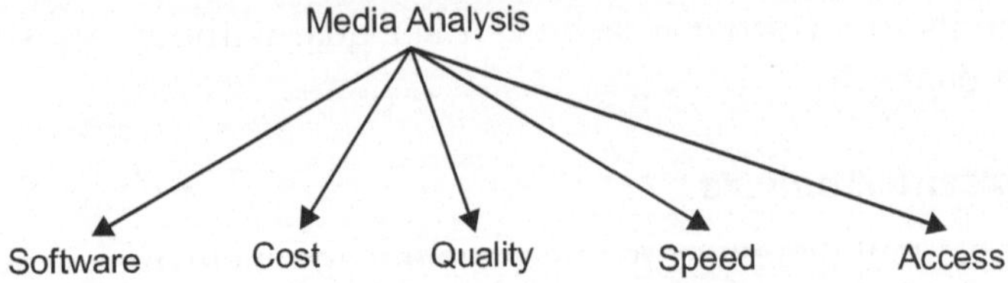


**Fig. 9.9. Learners' Media Analysis**

have access to a broadband network, graphics, simulation, other visual effects and synchronous and asynchronous communication. Instructional media makes learner with self-learning, self-confident and self-control.

### *Evaluation of Learners*

This evaluation of reaction is based on measurement of learners' feelings and opinions about the course after completed. The facilitator can get the information here relates to methods of instruction, course content, learning methods and materials. Behavioral changes of learners are a measurement of the behavioral changes occurring as a result of the learning event after completed.

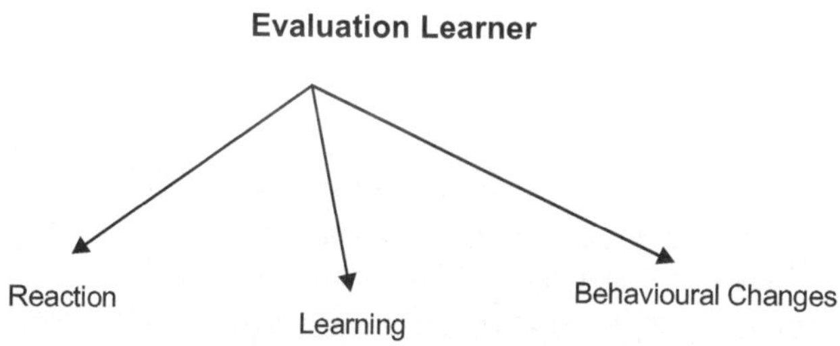


**Fig. 9.10. Learners' Evaluation**

### *Delivery Methodology*

The learning materials should be downloaded easily at learners place. The instructional media delivered with minimum space and maximum speed at learners' centre. The material and media should flexible to the learners' environment.

### *Revising Resources*

The facilitator can determine the ability of the web system to support the learner, the effectiveness of the learning environment, the effectiveness of the support offered to the learner, how web-based learning benefits when compared with the traditional methods. Based on the above findings of the evaluation changes may be needed to the learning methods and materials to support the learner.

## Conclusion

Methods and media play a major role in the success of a web-based learning process. Hence we need to assess the material and media to provide a better learning event. A web-based learning process cannot be successful without well-designing learning material, good facility support and assessment. Web-based learning is a self-based leaning and places the responsibility for study directly on the learners themselves. They need to know how to use the web based learning environment to be successful.

## REFERENCES

1. Bandura, A. (1986). *Social Foundations of Thought and Action: A Social Cognitive Theory*, Englewood Cliffs, NJ; Prentice Hall.
2. Weiner, B. (1992). *Human Motivation: Metaphors, Theories and Research*. Newbury Park, CA: Sage.
3. Wentzel, K. R. (1991). Relations Between Social Competence and Academic Achievement in Early Adolescence. *Child Development*, 62, 1066-1078.
4. Wentzel, K. R. (1994). Relations of Social Goal Pursuit to Social Acceptance, Classroom Behaviour and Perceived Social Support. *Journal of Educational Psychology*, 86, 173-182.
5. Wentzel, K. R. (1996). Social Goals and Social Relationships as Motivators of School Adjustment. In J.Juvonen, & K. R. Wentzel (Eds.), *Social Motivation: Understanding Children's School Adjustment* (pp. 226-247). New York: Cambridge University Press.

10

# Impact of Multimedia Technologies for Tamil Education

## *A Global Perspective*

— *Prof. B. Jagadhesan*

### Introduction

Tamil is a Dravidian language predominantly spoken in southern India and northeastern Sri Lanka, with smaller communities of speakers in many other countries. As one of the few living classical languages, Tamil has an unbroken literary tradition of over two millennia. The written language has changed little during this period, with the result that classical literature is as much a part of everyday Tamil as modern literature. Tamil school children, for example, are still taught the alphabet using the átticúdi, an alphabet rhyme written around the first century AD. Modern technologies have started changing the lifestyle of our modern population. Multimedia, as a teaching aid, is very much effective with colour, sound, graphics, which are found in the audio media and video media and movie media. One of the most significant changes in Tamil education in recent years has been the availability of a range of Information Communication

Technologies (Multimedia). Thus, Multimedia is no longer a new terminology nowadays. Almost everyone is familiar with Multimedia not only at work but also in schools as it encompasses the Internet and Multimedia.

The power of Multimedia can be used effectively in language teaching and learning as there is a paradigm shift from traditional teaching to using Multimedia in classrooms. It provides alternative teaching methods and it is a breakthrough from the traditional classroom environment. This is an efficient method to engage today's pupils. Multimedia tool is believed to provide the possibilities of multiple perspectives and a realistic learning environment. The real power of multimedia to improve education may only be realized when students actively use them as cognitive tool. Furthermore computer-based learning is more motivating for students and this is generally accepted by educators and by administrators. Special innovative method can be supported to the young learners acquiring more vocabularies for suitable communication transactions in Tamil.

The contents have been presented with an elaborate use of multimedia technologies. The lessons of the educational programmes have been made more interactive and illustrative through pictures, animations, video clippings and audio contents. The library presents a picture-gallery and a video gallery on a large number of cultural events, temples and historical monuments. It also presents the devotional songs in audio mode. This paper presents the impact and experiences of developing multimedia based online resource for Tamil Education and culture history and art for global perspective.

## Need of Multimedia in Teaching Tamil languages

Explore the possibilities of the effective use of Multimedia in imparting Tamil language education. Analyze the potential of 2D and 3D software, audio, video, comics, comic strips and motion pictures in the acquisition of Tamil language skills.

Identify the effective use of open source software and operating system for instructing Tamil language skills. Internet comprises innumerable features. It is the need of the hour to find out the means of using all those features for spreading the Tamil Language. Technological advancements in the field of 2D and 3D animations, Video, Audio, Comics, Comic stripes, Motion films have made the Tamil teaching incredibly easy. Software and operating systems like Ubuntu(Tamil Linux),Microsoft, Microsoft Tamil office, suratha Unicode writer and converter, Google search engine and guruji search engine etc have greatly helped for the development of Tamil language. Internet acts as bridge for connecting all the media together. In today's scenario, web blogs and social net working websites work as major sources of alternative Mass media. Web blogs and social networking web sites play a significant role in imparting Tamil education all over the world in different forms—audio, video, 2D, 3D and motion pictures, etc.

## Issues in Teaching Tamil

The main issue with teaching Tamil is lack of quality teachers. Even though there is some limited support from government for community languages, the lack of demand from the Tamil speaking population has meant very few schools offering Tamil lessons.

As far as Tamil is concerned there is no demand to employ a full time or part time Tamil teacher. The number of Tamil children in the school varies. if you look at the highly populated Asian community, there are community languages classes such as Urdu, Punjabi, and Arabic in the mainstream school. This is not only because of the number of students. At present Tamil is at the same stage in some countries. Efforts at developing a syllabus and teaching framework are underway. As you will all agree, a strong fundamental framework is a basis for a strong education system. This brings us to the role of multimedia in teaching and learning Tamil.

**Real Impact of Multimedia for Teaching Tamil Language**

The development of material that takes full advantage of computer-assisted learning used to be much more involved and typically employed interactive learning and Multimedia. A team comprising of interactive designers, graphic designers, programmers, testing team and a manager, usually develops such materials. A multimedia project may take up to six months of development time costing as much as $70 000. Despite this, not many commercial products seem to have a substantial shelf life. Many outstanding titles done by big companies like Broderbund are seemed irrelevant (content-wise) in many countries. Like most teaching resources, multimedia packages vary greatly in complexity, quality and perceived usefulness. As with most educational materials, there are many approaches to teaching a topic, and even a well-produced program is unlikely to satisfy everyone. Therefore such commercial titles are difficult, if not impossible, to be updated modified or improved by content experts for their specific needs. For that, the original programmer must be available to access the source code. Since the expertise to use new teaching tools stays with the IT developers, rather than with the teachers, the typical teacher makes little or no progress in the use of interactive media tools. To date there are less than 20 quality Tamil language based educational CD ROMs available worldwide. Most of these titles are produced in Malaysia. The content in these titles are based on the countries of their origin. Even though these titles score high in pedagogical value, the fact is there are still based on the local curriculum.

Authoring tools have improved rapidly. Some of these tools are easy to master. Time has come too drop the need for systems that make strong collaborations between IT Technicians and content experts (i.e. teachers). Now educationists can independently develop effective and customized instructional software for their own classrooms.

In the old days of programming, the developer had to everything in such arcane general purpose compiler languages like Assembler, Basic or C. However, now, many sophisticated resources are available readily. These include vast libraries of media, which can be copied and pasted in a program. Such clip-arts and sound clips are available on the Internet and CD ROM packages. There is also a range of tools available for each medium. From high-end professional packages to less sophisticated but still powerful and useful freeware offerings are available for the initiative programmer. The advent of easy-to-use multimedia authoring packages (like Mediator), and the widespread availability of computers, and the ease with which traditional classroom teaching can be put into instructional software have all created an environment in which, traditional classroom teaching can be transformed and made more exciting for students and teachers.

## Conclusion

The perennial problem faced by emigrant Tamil communities is getting quality resources to teach Tamil to the younger generation. Multimedia development has actually become quite easy. I hope that this chapter would inspire the audience to get together and develop their own multimedia teaching and learning pedagogical materials.

## REFERENCES

1. Karrer, T *Understanding e-Learning* 2.0
2. http://www.learningcircuits.org/2007/0707karrer.html
3. Nichols, M. *e-Learning in Context.*
4. http://akoaotearoa.ac.nz/sites/default/files/ng/group-
5. 661/n877-1—e-Learning-in-context.pdf
6. Turgut, Y., & Irgin, Pelin (2009). Young Learners' Language Games Learning via computer Games. Procedia Social and Behavioural Sciences 1 (2009) pp. 760-764 Vaughan, Taay. (1997). *Multimedia Making It Works.* (3rd edition) New Delhi: Tata McGraw Hill.

11

# Teaching Primary Education in Tamil Using LMS and Visualization Techniques

— *Richards Hadlee and R.E. Iniya Nehru*

**ABSTRACT**

*Extend teaching primary education in Tamil through Visualization technique. Visualization is creating images, diagrams, or animations to communicate a message. It's an effective way to communicate both abstract and concrete ideas. Visual representation of information requires merging of data, computer graphics, design, and imagination. Moodle provides only text information (report, items analysis, etc) and does not provide visualization tools. We use third-party tools to do visualization for LMS. Visualization helps to communicate results and understand better.*

**Keywords:** *Moodle, LMS, Visualization*

## Introduction and Purpose

LMS (Learning Management System) is highly interactive teaching tool. It offers great variety of workspaces to facilitate information sharing and communication among participants. It also provides a platform for a teacher to create/deliver contents, monitor student participation, and assess student performance through web application; this helps wider audience of students across the world (Education—Anytime and Anywhere). e-Learning classes most of the time is asynchronous. In this mode the instructor and students can interact via messaging or e-mail, and assignments can also submitted. The students and the instructor can be online at the same time to communicate directly and share information if required. e-Learning can include training, delivery of just-in-time information and guidance from Teacher.

A LMS (Learning Management System) is used to organize an online learning environment. The term 'online' refers to Internet and Intranet environments. It can include images, text, audio, video, animation and virtual environments. LMS and Visualization Techniques help to teach the primary school subjects by representing interactive or animated flash image files. The child chooses the learning style which has the seeing, feeling. Understanding learning styles is only a first step in maximizing potential and overcoming learning differences.

### Lists of Functionalities

- Creating LMS for Primary education
- Applying visualization
- Questions and log reports

***Creating LMS for Primary Education:*** This LMS has been designed for primary education (1st to 5th Standard) in Tamil language. Each standard has its own subjects (Tamil, Mathematics, Science, and Social Science). These contents have been designed using visualization techniques.

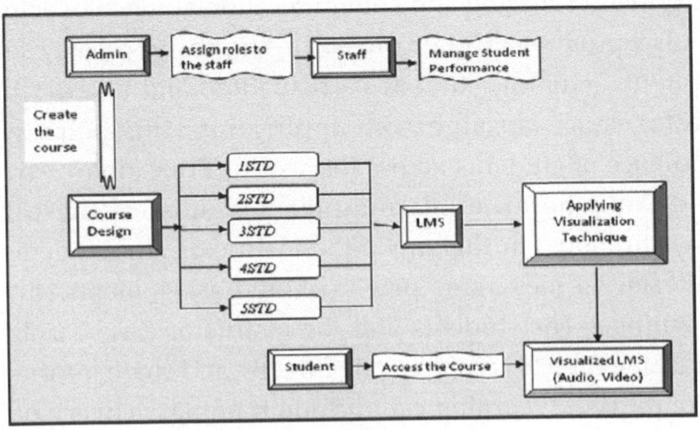


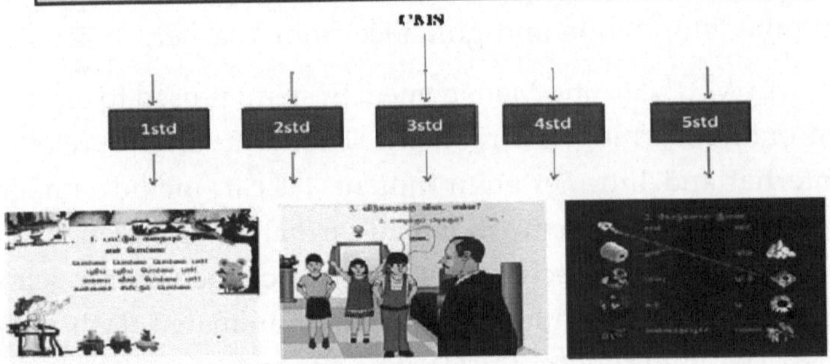


***Applying Visualization:*** Visualization is a branch of computer graphics which is concerned with interactive presentation/animated digital images for users to grasp easily. These techniques facilitate analysis of large information by representing visual display. The instructor and students can interact with forum, chat etc.

***Questions and Reports:*** Each lesson contains the various types of exercises, through which the user can perform exercises in an effective way. The grades are provided for the particular question which is performed by the user. The status of the question also is displayed at the end of the test. If the user answered correctly, right status is displayed and grade has been marked as 1/1. If the user selected the wrong answer, no grade is provided.

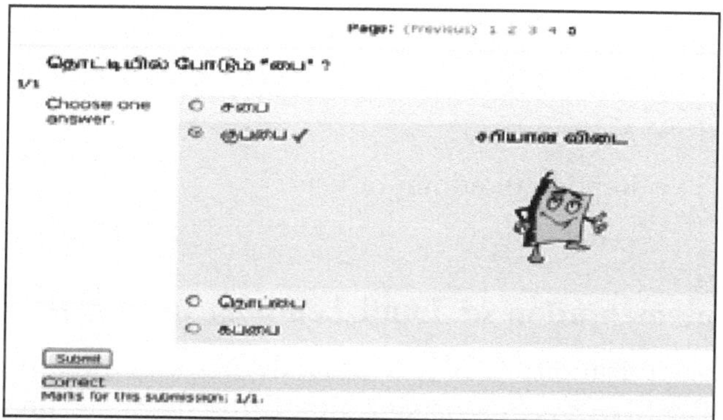


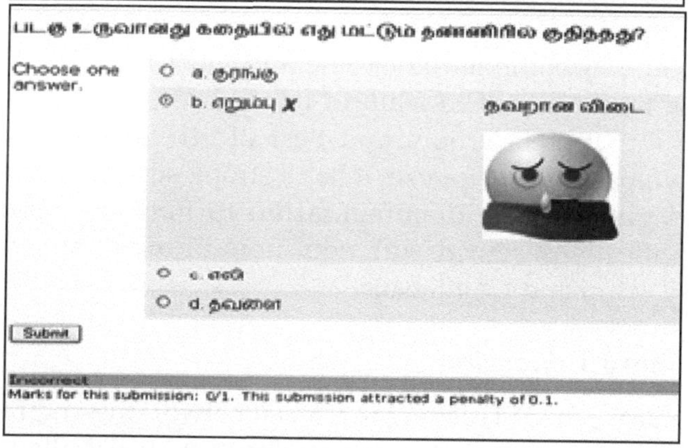


*Reports:* The Reports is represented through a visualized pattern (Graph). This contains the number of days the student has worked on this. In this graph the x-axis consists the date and month he worked in and the y-axis consists of the levels of work he has done on the particular day.

*Log Report:* Log Reports represents the lists of user who enroll into the particular course. Through this log the admin can get the performance of the user.

*Activity Report:* An activity report has the number of activity in that particular course. It contains the number of available resources for the course.

*Participants Report:* The Participants reports consists of the following criteria,

- What Activity?
- At what day?
- Reports of admin or user?
- What actions?

## Implementation of Tamil Learning in Moodle

This application has designed and developed through Moodle, PHP & MySql using Visualization Techniques. The purpose of this application is to bring awareness about e-Learning using Moodle. Moodle is the easiest and most flexible LMS. It's easy to navigate, had features that are directly applicable to the writing classroom and best of all, is free for me to download and customize. It has a strong support community and good online documentation to help us. Moodle is specifically designed with educators in mind, allowing for easy setup and maintenance.

### *Primary Education*

Primary School Teaching is a social networking and resource sharing site made exclusively for Teachers. It also allows other members of staff working in Primary Schools to participate. It is a platform for sharing teaching resources and ideas. It allows teachers to communicate effectively in a collaborative environment. Proof of that is, you will see many times a kid playing with his toys and imagine that he is in a battle field or a camp and they really feel it. All the subjects can be created with questions, so that the users get grade for any subject.

It is a process of transforming information into a visual form that enables user to observe the information. On the other side, it uses techniques of computer graphics and imaging. Successful visualizations can reduce the time to get the information, make sense, and enhance creative thinking.

We can use visualization for improving memory, restoring health, reducing stress, increasing relaxation.

The following properties are used in visualization

- Text
- Graphics
- Images
- Video
- Audio
- Animation

## Approach and Design

LMS and Visualization Techniques help to teach the primary school subjects by representing interactive or animated flash image files. Understanding learning styles is only a first step in e-Learning that overcome the learning differences. There is no doubt of the effectiveness of visualization in every area of life, even a child does visualization although they don't know what it is.

### *Resources*

The course has the lessons in it. The lists of resources are available in each lesson in the particular course. The lessons have been implemented in the tool called eXe. The eXe project developed a freely available Open Source authoring application to assist teachers and academics in the publishing of web content without the need to become proficient in HTML or XML markup. Resources authored in eXe can be exported in IMS Content Package, SCORM 1.2, or IMS Common Cartridge formats or as simple self-contained web pages. The content material in the particular lesson also been designed in Flash, in which a students can be attracted to learn difficult subjects through interactive audio and video based content. The LMS has also been implemented using Visualization and Computer graphics in order to improve the courses on the students learning in Tamil.

Three main uses of visualization are:

- Motivation. Creative visualization is a great way to see a possible future and move you towards it.
- Mental practice or rehearsal. Mental practice or mental rehearsal is complementary to real practice. Mental practice can also be cost-effective and safer.
- Reinforcing other techniques. Visualization is a powerful way to strengthen other techniques, such as association and scripting

## Conclusion

In this work we have shown application of teaching education in Tamil using LMS along with a visualization technique. We have described how different visualization techniques can be used in order to improve the courses on the students learning in Tamil. All these technique affiliated to the student's performance. The animated image avoids the monotonous feeling of reader which we normally get in classroom. Presently most of the children are computer friendly, spend lot of time in computer games, animation etc. Hence developing a course content using LMS tools like Moodle, PHP and MYSQL gives a different visual presentation to children. The students can be attracted to learn difficult subjects using Visualization and Computer graphics. The retention rate for an average student in found to be much more using LMS techniques compared to traditional classroom training.

## *Acknowledgment*

I express my sincere thanks to Mr. E. Iniya Nehru, Technical Director, NIC (Chennai) His encouragement and enthusiastic support throughout this paper induced me to do well. I also thank Mr. Jeyakumar S, the Project Manager at NIC who helped me to get the needed information and encouraged for successful completion of this paper.

## REFERENCES

**Book**

1. Using Moodle 2nd Edition, By Jason Cole and Helen Foster Published by O'Reilly Media, Inc, 1005 Grayenstein Highway North, Sebastopol, CA 95472

**Articles**

1. Factors in the deployment of a Learning management system at The University of the South Pacific Moodle For Teachers, Trainers And Administrators Moodle An Electronic Classroom

**Resources**

1. http://download.moodle.org/
2. http://exelearning.org/wiki
3. www.docebo.org

12

# Role of Cloud Computing in Tamil Language Development

— *Dr. Mrs. A. Pethalakshmi and Mrs. R. RajaRajeswari*

**ABSTRACT**

*Cloud Computing is a new computing paradigm which is expected to transform the way computing is done today, in near future. Cloud Computing offers virtualization of all high end Computing Services. And it offers four layers of Services: Saas (Software as a Service), PaaS (Platform as a Service), CaaS (Computing as a Service) and IaaS (Infrastructure as a Service). These services can cut the software cost, storage cost and utility cost of running a wide computer network. This research paper addresses how cloud computing can facilitate Tamil Language development. The following areas are identified as prospective avenues of development: e-Learning , Tamil Computing , Tamil e-Resources and Tamil Internet Services. This research paper will analyse the existing Tamil software services in the above said areas and explore these avenues of Tamil Development Through Cloud Computing.*

***(Keywords**: Cloud Computing, e-Learning, Tamil Computing, Tamil e-Resources)*

## Introduction

Forecast on Computing tells cloudy days are ahead for Computer Scientists. Software Developers and Users should be ready for a changeover as Cloud Computing waves roll down into the Internet. This new computing paradigm is expected to transform the style of computing in a remarkable way. Tamil, one of the world's five classical languages, is a privileged language, to be learnt by Lord Buddha[11]. Its history dates back to its existence on stone inscriptions in Jerusalem. This research paper tries to make these two ends meet *i.e.* how the new computing paradigm, cloud computing, can be connected with this historical language. This research paper is organized as follows: an introduction to cloud computing, avenues of Tamil Language Development facilitated by cloud computing and the final conclusion.

## An Insight Into Cloud Computing

Cloud Computing[8] is Internet-based computing, whereby shared resources, software and information are provided to computers and other devices on demand like a public utility. Cloud computing[9] is Internet-based ('Cloud') development and use of computer technology ('computing'). The cloud is a metaphor for the Internet-based on how it is depicted in computer network diagrams and is an abstraction for the complex infrastructure it conceals. According to a 2008 paper published by IEEE Internet Computing "Cloud Computing is a paradigm in which information is permanently stored in servers on the Internet and cached temporarily on clients that include desktops, entertainment centers, table computers, note books, wall computers, hand helds, sensors, monitors etc." Cloud computing offers virtualization of all high end services and it offers four layers of Services [1, 2, 4, 5, 6, 7].

### *Applications or Software as a Service*

SaaS means delivering software over the internet. This nullifies the need to install and run application on individual computers, making software upgrades, maintenance and support obsolete. (e.g) Salesforce.com

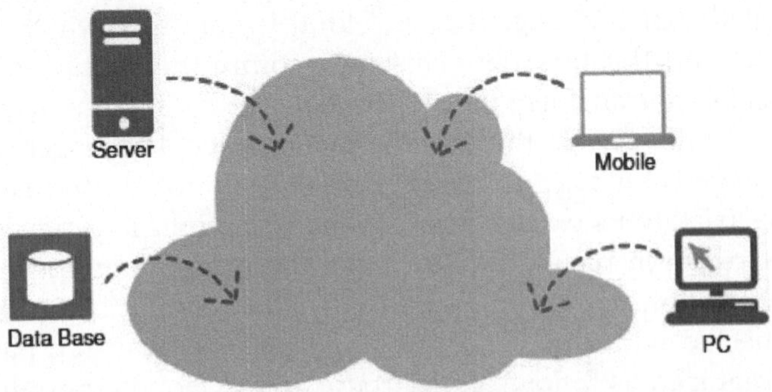


Courtesy : www.cloudtweaks.com
Fig.1

**Fig. 12.1.**

### *Platform as a Service*

PaaS is the delivery of a computing platform as a service. PaaS offerings facilitate deployment of application without the cost and complexity of buying and managing the underlying hardware and software and provisioning hosting capabilities. (*e.g*) Windows Azure, Amazon Elastic Computer Cloud.

### *Infrastructure as a Service*

IaaS is a provision model is which an organization outsources the equipment used to support operations, including storage, hardware, servers and networking components. The service provider owns the equipment and is responsible for housing, running and maintaining it. The client typically pays on a peruse basis. (*e.g*) Amazon S3

### *Computing as a Service*

CaaS[1] integrates the above said services. (*e.g*) Verizon's CaaS. Like other cloud offerings, Verizon's CaaS allows customers pay for data-center resources such as storage and application hosting dynamically based on the amount of resources they consume. These services can cut the software cost, storage cost and utility cost of running a wide network. The following sections bridges Cloud Computing Services and Tamil Language Development in prospective avenues.

## Tamil e-Resources

Literary Resources in a language symbolizes its richness and liveliness. Now in this internet age, e-mail box has replaced the conservative letter box in a house. Hence E-resources have a definite role in making a language flourish. Internet has paved a way for Tamil Internet magazines, e-books and also a Tamil electronic libray (www.tamilelibrary.org). For example, www.projectmadurai.com plays a major role in the area of e-documentation of old Tamil literature. One has free access to Tamil Literature in this website from 'Abirami Anthathi' to 'Alai Osai'. Apart from this, many Tamil magazines have their own websites comprising even digital archives of old ones. (*e.g*) www.vikatan.com. Also any creator's work needs to be published and recognised, for both the growth of the language and the creator.

Tamil Internet magazines act as writer's workshops, for budding Tamil writers from which they can learn and also where they can publish their work. (*e.g.*) www.thinnai.com, www.nilacharal.com. With the advent of Cloud Computing, usage of IaaS can cut storage costs, emancipating separate clouds for old Tamil Literature, Magazines and modern Tamil Literature. Such e-Resources available on the Internet facilitate free access to Tamil Literature for any one across the globe, which is a requisite for a language to grow.

## Tamil e-Learning

Tamil community has settled across the globe even many decades before. And there is need to teach Tamil for the next generation young learners to keep the tamil heritage and language expand its horizon. Internet takes the avatar of a virtual Guru for this purpose. "International Academy for Internet Tamil "Formerly, Tamil Virtual University (www.tamilvu.org)does this job with ease in colloboration with Tamil University, Thanjavur and awards Degrees, Certificates and Diplomas in Tamil for Tamil learners across the globe through Internet.

Virtual Classroom, a part of this academy's website, which transits the learner from the living room into a class room needs additional software in a Remote terminal, *e.g.* Multimedia Software. Using PaaS,this software can be downloaded and any remote user can turn the terminal into a virtual class room. And apart from this enlightening Video lectures by eminent Tamil Professors will reach across the globe when available as AaaS for enthusiastic learners.

### Tamil Internet Services

Twenty first century is the century of Information and Communication Technology. At the click of a mouse, Internet provides both communication in its highest speed and information in its best shade, at any moment. Searching for Tamil web pages is mostly done in English and only some Tamil search Engines like www.googletamil.com. does this job in Tamil that too using transliteration method. Tamil email software like www.azhahi.com though exist are not popularly used by tamil population. Since personal and official communication is under the process of transformation from letters to mails, sending mails in mother tongue will be a necessity among users who have a fast pace of life, to share their true emotions. Apart from this, a language should be put into use in all forms of communication by that language speaking people for its longevity and the one not, can exist only in books and stone inscriptions. And CaaS comes as a help at this moment for the software developers to develop next generation Tamil search Engines and Tamil e-mail sending software. Required Infrastructure, Platform, and Computing for developing these software can be got from IaaS, PaaS and CaaS providers respectively.

## Tamil Computing

Tamil Computing provides Tamil software tools which are used in a day to day basis. (*e.g.*) Tamil word processors, Tamil Database software like Amudham These tools need to get popularised and put into use by software users. Also Tamil Speech Recognition software is yet to come. To develop Tamil Speech Recognition Software more computing power is needed. To develop or run Speech Recognition applications, because of digital filtering and signal processing high processing speed and more memory are required[3]. And cloud computing comes handy by providing them through CaaS, since cloud computing transforms a desktop into a super computer. To help website developers develop tamil websites easier, Tamil website design templates can be made available as AaaS .

## Conclusion

Tamil is a unique language, an universal language, whose literature suits mankind of all centuries, all places and all tribes.[10] states that context sensitive rules of modern computer science are found in Tholkaapiyam,a classical literature. This language has undergone transformations, its storage from stone inscriptions to palm leaves, paper and now Web pages.

For a language to live long, it should be spoken without the acquaintance of any foreign language. Today's tamil language is spoken along with many english words. In spite of this, this language is ever young and vibrant and can be symbolised as a wild flower which blossoms in a natural way. Hence this language will evolve with any emerging technology and tamil language can develop in the above said avenues through cloud computing services.

## REFERENCES

1. http://connectedplanetonline.com
2. http://edgewatertech.wordpress.com
3. http://www.faqs.org/docs/Linux/SpeechRecognition .Howto.html
4. http://www.scribd.com
5. http://searchcloudcomputing.techtarget.com
6. http://universitybusiness.com
7. http://web2.sys.con.com
8. en.wikepedia.org
9. Dr. Durgesh Pant *et.al*, Cloud Computing, CSI Communication, January 2009.
10. Dr. Gift Siromeny, Context Sensitive Rules in Tolkappiam, *Proceedings of the Second World Tamil Conference*,1968.
11. News, Makkal TV, January 2009.

13

# Information Retrieval System for Tamil and Non-Tamil Users

— S. Srividhya and Dr. T. Mala

*ABSTRACT*

*This scheme enhances a remarkable approach to formulate and expand query. It accepts query given by user and expands it through a series of query expansion techniques. The input given by user is Tamil text and the output is expanded query to be given to a search engines to retrieve relevant English documents.*

***Keywords***— *Word Sense Disambiguation, Word Stemming, Transliteration.*

## Introduction

The World Wide Web (WWW), a rich source of information is growing at an enormous rate. According to Online Computer Library Centre, English is still the dominant language in the web that contributes most of the content. However, global internet usage statistics reveal that the number of non-English internet users is steadily on the rise, but all of them are not able to express their basic needs in English. Tamil users who are not able to express their needs in English are also growing in the Internet. They generally search for the information using the Tamil search engines. But the content provided by these search engines is less in number. Making the huge repository of information on the translation module takes the stemmed word web, which is available in English, accessible to non-English internet users has become an important challenge in recent times. When the non-English users want to access the existing search engines, most of the time they arrive at improper formulation of English queries. The proposed system aim to solve the above problem by allowing the users to pose the query in their own (source) language which is different from the language of the documents that are searched. This enables users to express their information need in their native language while the proposed system takes care of expanding the given user query that can be given to Search engines like Google, Alta vista.

## Literature Survey

"Query formulation for Information Retrieval System for Tamil Users" seeks to develop efficient techniques for query formulation whose accuracy and precision are determined by parameters like precision and recall. The query formulation process is broadly divided into three main portions: word stemming, translation and word sense disambiguation. The Word stemming is done with a morphological analyzer whose source code is modified to perform word stemming. The input is got in UNICODE and converted to TAB-Anna font. The translation module takes the stemmed word as input and transliterates those words to as input and transliterates those words to English and the equivalent English words Bilingual dictionary is developed for this purpose. The word sense disambiguation makes use of Bootstrap algorithm[3] which disambiguates 55 per cent of the words with 92 per cent accuracy. CLIR system for Agricultural society[8]: Tamil-English CLIR system for agricultural society uses Lesk algorithm for word sense disambiguation which is only 44 per cent accurate and the Tamil words from the input query is directly searched in bilingual dictionary without checking for spelling mistakes. Information retrieval system using mobile networks[5]: This system needs user interaction to disambiguate the word and the translation is prone to ambiguities if the context is not clearly specified by the user.

Cross Lingual Information Retrieval Using Data Mining Methods[6]: In this system the feedback and suggestions from the users are collected for document mapping. For each candidate word the pair wise measure gives a measure of correlation. However, these correlations are not available in dictionary representations and must be generated by use of appropriate ontological systems. Tamil search engine[2]: This system discuss the issues related to crawler, database storage structure and other functional modules of the search engine. While they have shown some limited success, the approach used by the search engine is limited to the Tamil language and it retrieves the Tamil documents.

## System Architecture

The system architecture is shown in Figure 13.1. The system mainly focuses on the construction of suitable English and the equivalent English words are fetched from a bilingual dictionary.. query for relevant English document retrieval in an information retrieval system. The proposed system gets Tamil input and retrieves relevant English documents according to the user query. The query is then given to spell checker. Morphological Analyzer obtains the root terms of source query by removing grammatical inflections. By applying rules for handling suffices, oblique, etc., the root words are obtained in the given query. Transliteration is done to convert Tamil letters to English characters in a systematic way. The output is then disambiguated to find out the exact equivalent English word. Word sense disambiguation is done that identifies the correct sense of an ambiguous word that is being used in a query.

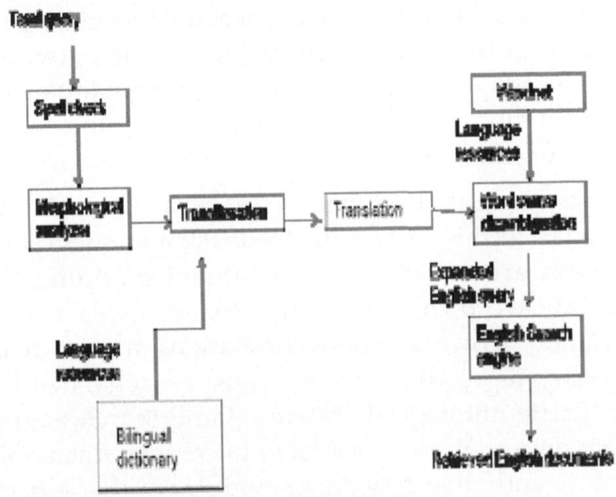


**Fig. 13.1 : Word Sense Disambiguation**

Translation is part of word sense disambiguation. For each sense of a given word, it is compared with all possible senses of the surrounding words in the given query and the word with maximum senses is chosen as the appropriate word. With the exact English words obtained as a result of word sense disambiguation, query formulation is done and given to search engines for English documents retrieval. If Tamil query is entered, the grammatical inflections are removed using morphological analyzer and query is formulated to retrieve relevant Tamil documents. WordNet, dictionary are the resources used. The formulated query is given to an existing search engine like Google, Alta vista. It uses bootstrap algorithm for Word sense disambiguation.

Bootstrap algorithm for Word sense disambiguation: Bootstrapping algorithm for Word Sense Disambiguation succeeds in disambiguating a subset of the words in the input text with very high precision. It uses WordNet as resource to disambiguate and for the purpose of identifying the correct sense of the words in a given text. The bootstrapping process initializes a set of ambiguous words with all the nouns and verbs in the text. It then applies various disambiguation procedures and builds a set of disambiguated words: new words are sense tagged based on their relation to the already disambiguated words, and then added to the set. This process allows us to identify, in the original text, a set of words which can be disambiguated with high precision; 55 per cent of the verbs and nouns are disambiguated with an accuracy of 92 per cent.

## Evaluation Parameters

### *Precision*

In the field of information retrieval, precision is the fraction of retrieved documents that are relevant to the search:

$$\text{precision} = \frac{[(\text{relevant document}) \cap (\text{retrieved documents})]}{[(\text{retrieved documents})]}$$

### *Recall*

Recall in Information Retrieval is the fraction of the documents that are relevant to the query that are successfully retrieved.

$$\text{recall} = \frac{[(\text{relevant document}) \cap (\text{retrieved documents})]}{[(\text{relevant documents})]}$$

For example for text search on a set of documents recall is the number of correct results divided by the number of results that should have been returned. The precision and recall values for five different queries have been calculated as follows:

| Precision | 0.72 | 0.89 | 0.78 | 0.76 | 0.80 |
|---|---|---|---|---|---|
| Recall | 0.77 | 0.86 | 0.84 | 0.78 | 0.82 |

## Conclusion

The proposed System helps to find links of documents for health society and to retrieve the documents from a large corpus in English language. This system is very much useful for the users who can understand English but do not know to give appropriate English query. The users can pose their query in Tamil and retrieve relevant English documents by using this system. The Query formulation for information retrieval system for Tamil users displays the search result in English. It is appropriate, if the results are displayed in their own language for the users who do not know how to give query in English.

The precision can be improved by employing Machine translation methods instead of word-by-word translation technique. The bilingual dictionary can be extended to include more words which will expand the scope of the system. This system can be further extended to Rank the pages and provide a summary (in English) of top pages, translate the summary to Tamil or provide an answer to the query in Tamil.

## REFERENCES

1. Anand Kumar M, Dhanalakshmi V, Rajendran S, Soman K, "A Novel Approach to Morphological Analysis for Tamil Language", *Proceedings of the Tamil Internet Conference*, 2009, pp.244 - 249.
2. Baskaran Sankaran. "*Tamil Search Engine*", Tamil Internet, California, U.S.A, 2002.
3. Rada F.Mihalcea & Dan I. Moldovan," A Highly Accurate Bootstrap Algorithm for Word Sense Disambiguation", *International Journal on Artificial Intelligence Tools*, 2001, Vol.10, No. 1-2.
4. M.B.A.Salai Aaviyamma and Dr.K.Kathiravan," Problems related to English-Tamil Translation", *Proceedings of the Tamil Internet Conference*, 2009, pp. 169-172.
5. R. Shriram & Vijayan Sugumaran, "Cross Lingual Information Retrieval and Delivery Using Community Mobile Networks", IEEE, 2006.

6. R.Shriram&Vijayan Sugumaran,"Cross Lingual Information Retrieval Using Data Mining Methods", *Americas Conference on Information Systems* (AMCIS), 2009
7. Sinnathurai Srivas," Inside Tamil Unicode", *Proceedings of the Tamil Internet Conference*, 2009, pp. 140-144.
8. D.Thenmozhi and C. Aravindan, "Tamil-English Cross Lingual Information Retrieval System for Agriculture Society", *Proceedings of the Tamil Internet Conference*, 2009, pp. 173-178.
9. Dr. Vasu Renganathan, "*An Interactive Approach to Development of English-Tamil*
10. Machine Translation System on the Web", *Proceedings of the Tamil Internet Conference*, California, U.S.A, 2002.

14

# Searchko
## *The King of Search for Tamil Web Documents*

— *Sobha Lalitha Devi, Pattabhi R.K. Rao T. and Vijay Sundar Ram R.*

**ABSTRACT**

*Searchko is a Tamil portal, which uses information retrieval (IR) technology for searching the Tamil content in the web. The Searchko engine uses many types of natural language processing technology for getting the most relevant output. The web has nearly 10 million documents in Tamil and bringing it under one umbrella using IR technology is the aim of Searchko. The etimology of searchko is Search+Ko ie search+ king, ko in Tamil means king and thus this portal is a unique portal where you can get all the content , whether it is News from the Newspapers, Cinema, Tamil literature, Music and Cricket. The unique features of SearchKo are Multiple Font support, enhancing the query with the help of a morph analyzer, Works with a phonetic visual keyboard, Spell Checking, Query expansion using thesaurus and dictionaries.*

## Introduction

The growth of technology and Internet has brought information revolution in our country and across the world. This 21st century is called as information age. This has changed the way people share the knowledge, do business, and interact with each other. Until 1990's Internet was dominated by only English content. Today the World Wide Web has grown wider and has become very large, having content in all Indian languages. And especially in Tamil, web has more than 10 million documents. With this huge amount of Tamil data available on web, we require systems which will enable users to easily search and access data. In the present chapter we present a description of Searchko, a Tamil portal, whose objective is to provide Tamil users access to all Tamil content on web.

## Searchko—An Overview

Searchko provides various contents for the users. The search contents are classified into different domains such as Literature, Health, and Cinema search. The content for health domain is created in-house from the health texts. The results obtained for health search are classified into allopathy, siddha, homoeopathy, ayurveda, when presented to the user. For example users interested in reading articles related to cancer, can give query as 'puRRu noy' and obtain documents from ayurveda, allopathy, homoeopathy, siddha. In the literature search, we can have focused search on contents of Tamil literatures of wide range from sangam literature to 20th century creations. This includes 'aimperum kaappiyam', 'ettuth thokai', devotional literatures such as 'kuravanji paatalkal', 'pakthi ilakkiyangkal', text having poems by Sidhars such as 'sidhar paatalkal' and present days kalki and jayakanthan stories. The content for general search consists news articles from online news magazines, Tamil wikipedia, blog sites and other Tamil sites. All these contents are crawled and indexed by search engine regularly and updated periodically. This process is fully automated. It has been observed that even though we have huge content in web in Tamil, people are not able to have access for these documents because most of the content is not available for search. By developing this portal we have made all the Tamil content on web accessible to the users.

Another important feature is the lexical resource most often referred by people of all age groups as dictionaries is available for search and there are English-Tamil, Tamil- English dictionaries. We have found that there are different online dictionaries available in the web, but most of these do not provide the exact meaning of words in all senses. For example for the word 'bank', There are different noun senses and verb senses such as 'financial institution', 'river bank', "to take support on someone or something". Searchko provides online dictionaries, where all senses of the word are given along with the word's part-of-speech category. The user interface of the dictionaries is very simple and user friendly.

English-Tamil dictionary consists of more than 150000 root words. And similarly Tamil-English dictionary consists of more than 100000 words. The Tamil-English dictionary also includes old Tamil words, for which finding meanings in today's new dictionaries is quiet difficult. The English-Tamil dictionary includes Technical terms also. These dictionaries were created by lexicographers and verified by linguistic experts. These are very helpful to Translators.

Searchko provides entertainment contents focussing cinema, music and sports. In Cinema section, we provide details of actors, film directors, music directors, playback singers, and producers for each Tamil film. The Cinema database is updated whenever a new film is released. Users can search by giving actors names or film names or music director's names or producer's names. For example if the user searches for actor 'Rajnikanth', the Cinema search provides all films acted by Rajnikanth, for each film of his, will be provided with details of producer's name, director's name, playback singers name, Date of film release and also will fetch a relevant video of the film from You tube, if it exists. This cinema section also provides users with list of new upcoming films, their promotional videos if it exists. This can be considered as Tamil IMDB.

The music section of the portal is focussed on music festival of 'markazhi' month (Dec -Jan) also known 'markazhi thiruvizhaa' at Chennai. Here we provide schedules of all music events that take place in various auditoriums or 'sabhas' in and around Chennai. The schedules can be searched based on date or artist name or auditorium name or by time of event. The music lovers of the city have found this very helpful as they can find the time and venue of their interested event. This section also provides devotional hymns of Tiruppavai, Tiruvembavai and Tirupalliezuchi along with their meanings in Tamil. These devotional hymns are sung commonly during this markazhi month in various temples and households of Tamil Nadu.

In the Searchko, we provide live cricket scorecard in Tamil. The Cricket scorecard in English is obtained from websites such as cricinfo, cricbuzz, willow, and these scores are translated on-line to Tamil. The translation is done automatically. Here we use template based extraction and translation. For translating names of players, we use transliteration engine. The transliteration engine is built using statistical methodology[1]. The engine is trained using a parallel named entity lexicon. The engine works with an accuracy of 93 per cent. The content in the whole web portal is fetched and displayed automatically without any manual intervention. The Natural language processing modules of Searchko. Searchko has many unique features, which are developed using sophisticated natural language processing techniques.

### *Multiple Fonts Encoding Support*

Tamil content on web are in various encoding schemes and not as in English. There is a large data available in proprietary fonts. On giving a query the system searches all the Tamil pages independent (covering most of the proprietary fonts) of fonts to get the relevant pages. And snippets for all the retrived documents are given in Unicode. To achieve this font independency in the search engine, we have used different transcoder engines to unify the contents in to Unicode. A font transcoder engine identifies the encoding scheme of one font and makes an equivalent map to another font encoding scheme. Here we have converted all proprietary fonts into UTF-8 encoding scheme. For the purpose ofm creating equivalent map, both encoding schemes have to be analysed and each glyph of proprietary font has to be mapped to the Unicode scheme. There can be one to many or many to one mapping.

### *Enhancing the query with the help of a morph analyzer*

Tamil being a morphologically rich language, multiple words can be generated from a given root word. For *e.g.* the word 'padi' will have words like 'padithaan', 'padiththaal' etc. Here in our search engine, we enhance the query with the help of a morphological analyzer to retrieve all documents which have the various forms of the given query word. A morphological analyzer is a language processing tool, which will segment a given word into root word and it suffixes and will give their syntactic information respectively. .

Example 'viitukal' -> 'viitu' + 'kal'

Here in this task, the morphological analyzer is used only to get the root word. This is done using Finite State Automata and paradigm based approach[4]. This works with an average precision of 92.13 per cent. For example if the query word is 'malarkal' the search engine will look for documents having words such as 'malar', 'malarkalai' 'malarai', etc. This enables the user to give a query in crisp and easy form and get retrieved documents having all possible forms of the query word.

## *Query expansion using thesaurus and dictionaries*

We use a Tamil thesaurus and dictionary to retrieve more documents with the same sense. This increases the relevant documents[2]. For example, for the query word 'puu', documents are searched for other words with same sense like 'malar', 'pushpam', 'alar', 'koNtai', 'sutaan' along with the given query word 'puu'. The thesaurus is an advanced form of a lexicon, which contains the root words and their synsets in contrast to a lexicon which contain meaning and pronunciation of words. Here we have used a electronic thesaurus, which contains synsets of the root words. The thesaurus and the dictionary contain around 75000 words. This resource is increased as and when we encounter new words. Here the search handles AND, OR and Quoted queries.

## *Works with a phonetic and on screen keyboard*

The main hinder for Tamil usage in Internet is keying the Tamil words. Here we have give two ways to input the Tamil query word. One for the users comfortable with keyboard, a phonetic keyboard and an on-screen keyboard for people comfortable with mouse. Using the phonetic key board Tamil words can be keyed in by keying the English alphabets in correspondence with Tamil phone. Example

அம்மா is keyed in by tying 'a' 'm' 'maa'.

In the on-screen keyboard all the letter and the glyphs used in Tamil are presented in a palette, as shown in the

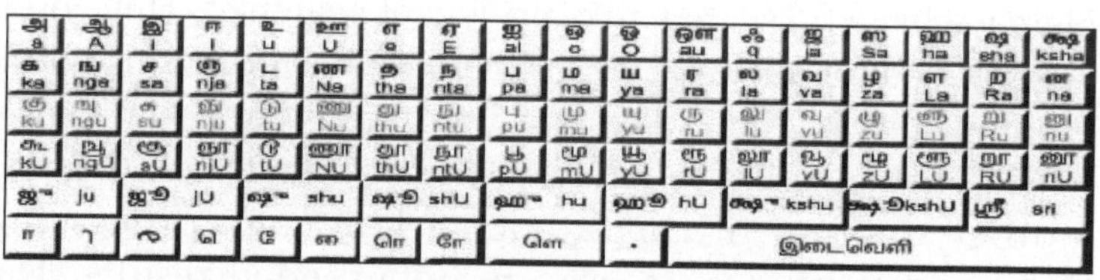

**Fig. 14.1. On-Screen KeyBoard**

Figure 14.1. By clicking the corresponding glyphs the query words are keyed in.

### *Spell Checking*

We check the spelling of the input query. This is the first search engine for India languages with integrated spell check facility. The spell checker checks the query word and suggests possible words for error words. The spell checker is developed using Finite State Automata (FSA), which is popular for accurate and speed performance[3]. Here we have used corpus based methodology for validating the correctness of the words. The FSA is built is using individual letters of the words. The spell checker validates 10 words in less than a millisecond. For example if the given query word is பதிணம் which is wrongly keyed in for, the suggested words are: 'திணம்' , 'புதிணம்' , 'ஆதிணம்' , 'பதிம்'

### Evaluation

The search results have been evaluated using standard Information Retrieval metrics of MAP, P@10. For the evaluation purpose 25 test queries were taken and the results obtained are checked for relevance by comparing with the expected results as given by human evaluator. We obtained evaluation results as follows. The MAP score we got is 0 .6 and P@10 (precision at 10) is 0.75 (i.e., for 10 documents we get 7.5 documents as relevant).

### Conclusion

Here we have presented an overview of Searchko. This portal is dedicated for all Tamil people across the world. This portal is completely in Tamil. The user interface is very easy to use, which enables users to navigate the web in Tamil, their on mother tongue. In this advance language processing technologies have been used to obtain good results. The search is available at http://www.searchko.in.

## REFERENCES

1. Mohammad Afraz and Sobha L (2008), 'English To Dravidian Language Machine Transliteration: A Statistical Approach Based On N-Grams', *In the Proceedings of International Seminar on Malayalam and Globalization*, Trivandrum, Kerla.
2. Pattabhi R. K. Rao and Sobha L (2008), "AU-KBC FIRE2008 Submission—Cross Lingual Information Retrieval Track: Tamil-English", *First Workshop of the Forum for Information Retrieval Evaluation* (FIRE), Kolkata. pp 1-5.
3. Vijay Sundar Ram R., Chandra Mouli N., Bhuvaneswari P., Ananda Priya J. and Kumara Shanmugam B. (2005), "Hybrid Approach for Developing a Tamil Spell Checker", In the *Proceedings of International Conference on Natural Language*, Indian Institute of Technology, Kanpur, pp. 111-115.
4. Vijay Sundar Ram R., Menaka S., and Sobha Lalitha Devi. (2010). "Tamil Morphological Analyser", In the *Proceedings of Knowledge Sharing Event on Morphological Analysers and Generators*, LDC-IL, CIIL, Mysore. pp 1-18.

# 15

# CoRe
## A Framework for Concept Relation-based Advanced Search Engine

— T. V. Geetha, Ranjani Parthasarathi
and Madhan Karky

**ABSTRACT**

*The number of Tamil documents is growing rapidly every second. Blogs, news portals, infonets and socialnets have considerably contributed to this growth. Traditional keyword based searches such as Google or Bing, primarily developed for English are now being used to search Tamil documents. These search engines do not have a full-fledged support for Tamil language. We present CoRe, the world's first framework for a concept relation based search engine for Tamil. CoRe search, unlike traditional keyword based searches, identifies the concepts in a document and their relationship with each other using UNL (Universal Networking Language). UNL is essentially a semantic relation based intermediate representation that has been used in this work for search index representation. This chapter presents the primary components of the CoRe framework, namely, EnCoRe (enconverter), CoReX (indexer) and CoReS (Search & Rank) modules. The CoRe based search is tested with over 50,000 crawled web documents and the results are compared against a traditional keyword based search algorithm over the same set of documents. It is observed that the UNL based search has a precision accuracy of 75 per cent.*

## Introduction

With UNICODE being accepted internationally as a standard for representing text on web sites, search engines are now indexing the pages independent of the language. Popular search engines like Google, Bing and Yahoo now readily index Tamil documents. Only Google manages to include certain language dependent features such as stemmer for Tamil. Even though keyword based search seems very convenient system to retrieve web documents it fails in two major issues. The first one is in understanding the document. The second one is in understanding what the user wants.

Let us start with a very simple example where a user wants to know about a temple in the city of Madurai. The user who does not know the actual name of the temple will use keywords Madurai and Temple in a search engine, which is very likely to retrieve documents that have mentions of both these keywords. What the traditional search engine will not be able to retrieve are documents that talk about Meenakshi temple which do not contain any of the search keywords. This failure of traditional search engine expects the user to reach these documents in their second or third search attempts with different keywords.

Personalised search engines aim to solve this problem from the user side. Concept based search engines aim to solve the same problem from both the ends. In this chapter we propose CoRe, a framework for a Concept—Relation Based Search. The CoRe framework aims at understanding the web documents by indexing them based on concepts and their relations rather than indexing the keywords and their frequencies. The framework was implemented and tested with over 50,000 documents from tourism domain. The search results were compared against traditional keyword based search for precision and relevance.

This chapter is recognize into five sections. The second section provides a brief survey of literature relevant to concept based search subsystems. The third section presents the CoRe framework and its components. The fourth section discusses the results of CoRe search engine and compares it against traditional keyword based search for precision and relevance. The fifth section summarises the paper, presents the work in progress and discusses future directions.

**Background**

Meaning based or concept based search and indexing techniques have been proposed for English and other languages. The main purpose of such indexing techniques is cross lingual information retrieval.

Universal Networking Language (UNL), proposed in our CoRe framework for enconversion of Tamil documents, is described in[3]. UNL is an Interlingua framework that was originally designed to aid the machine translation process[3]. An UNL enconverter interprets natural language and converts it into an intermediate representation that utilizes language independent semantic concepts and relations prescribed by UNL. The enconversion from the source language to UNL analyses the source language and utilizes language specific linguistic rules for building the UNL representation. On the other hand the UNL deconverter transforms UNL representation to a target language. For this purpose the deconverter uses language specific generation rules to produce the target language. Kang in[4] proposes a indexing technique where he indexes documents based on the concepts identified in the document. A similar work where medical images are conceptually indexed can be found in[5]. Chau and Yeh in[2] propose another conceptual index again based on concepts. Here Chau and Yeh have designed the index especially for cross lingual text retrieval. Surve et al.,[7] propose AgroExplorer, a meaning based multi lingual search system. Though these systems have the advantage of concept based indexing they do not investigate deep into the relations between the concepts in a sentence.

## CoRe Search Framework

CoRe search framework presented in figure 15.1 *(See next page)* It can be divided into two major divisions, online and offline, in terms of the time of processing. Three major subsystems EnCoRe, CoReX and CoReS form the backbone of the framework providing the major functionality. Tamil language tools are separated from rest of the system to offer language dependent services such as analysers and generators. This section describes the various components of the framework in detail.

### *Offline Processing*

The offline mode comprises of operations related to crawling Tamil web documents relevant to a particular domain, processing the raw document for extracting sentence constituents, converting the sentence constituents to corresponding UNL graphs and building the concept relation index. This is a periodic scheduled process and will be modifying the index incrementally as new documents are being crawled.

### *Online Processing*

A user's query is processed, expanded and converted to UNL graph(s) and sent to a search and ranking subsystem where the documents that match concept relation similarity are ranked and sent for output processing. The output processing module formats the output, generates snippets and summary for the retrieved documents and sends it to the user.

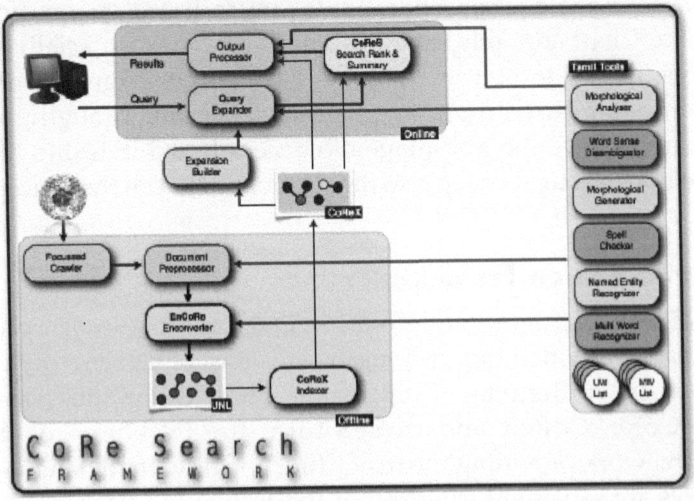


**Fig. 15.1. CoRe Search Framework**

## *Tamil Tools*

The Tamil tools package offers a set of language processing services for different components of the CoRe framework. Morphological Analyser[1] is used by most of the components for morphologically recognize a word. The rules for the EnCoRe subsystem depend on the results of the morphological analysis. Word Sense Disambiguator(WSD), a rule based tool, is used to resolve the meaning of a word based on it's context. This tool is used both by EnCoRe and Query Expander. Morphological Generator is used for generating natural language sentences. Output Processor uses Morphological Generator to generate natural language summary for a given document. Query Expander and EnCoRe use spell checker to auto correct typos and basic morphological errors. Named Entity Recogniser and Multiword Recogniser are used to identify named and multiword entities respectively. These rule based tools are used by EnCoRe and Query Expander to identify entities. The Tamil Tools also comprises of a Universal Word list (UW list)[3] and a Multiword List (MW list). These lists carry the domain related UW and MW words respectively.

### *Focussed Crawler*

Tamil web documents specific to a certain domain are fetched into the system by a Focused crawler. The domain specific words are fed to the crawler along with a seed URL list. The documents fetched by the crawler are sent to the Document Pre-processor for further processing.

### *Document Pre-processor*

Document Pre-processor parses Tamil documents in HTML format for textual content removing links and other unwanted tags. The Pre-processor also identifies important sentence constituents and send the sentence constituent along with a document id to the EnCoRe subsystem.

### *EnCoRe*

The EnCoRe subsystem forms the heart of the CoRe framework. Here a sentence constituent is passed to a rule based system to identify the various concepts in the constituent and the rules are used to identify one of the 44 UNL relations[3]. EnCoRe uses language processing tools such as the Morphological Analyser to [ecognize various morphological suffices of a word and uses this information along with syntax and semantics to identify the relationship between concepts. UNL graphs are generated for every sentence constituent. The UNL graph is then sent to CoReX indexer along with information such as document ID, positional index and original keyword, its frequency in the document etc. to be used by the CoReS subsystem.

### *CoReX Indexer*

The CoRex Indexer subsystem presented in[6] stores and manages the UNL graphs in three different indices. Concept only index(C index), Concept-Relation index (CR index) and

Concept-Relation-Concept index (CRC index) are the three indices maintained by the CoReX indexer. The UNL graphs are stored in the indices by their concept ids for efficient retrieval. The CoReX index structure and efficiency analysis is provided in[6].

### *Query Expander and Expansion Builder*

Any user query is directly sent to the Query Expander module that expands the query using the data from Expansion Builder. The Expansion Builder uses the CoReX index to build on-the-fly similarity thesaurus and co-occurrence list. Query Expander enconverts the user query to a UNL graph for the CoReS subsystem, using the information provided by the Expansion builder.

### *CoReS*

CoReS subsystem provides the CoRe framework with the functionality of searching and ranking documents based on concepts and relations. Unlike traditional algorithms that scores pages based on terms and their frequencies, CoReS subsystem ranks a document based on the concepts and the type of relations that exist between those concepts.

### *Output Processor*

Results from CoReS subsystem would be a set of documents and their corresponding weight with respect to the user query and expansions. Output processor formats the result page by generating snippets highlighting the identified concepts and also generates a template-based summary for every page. For instance in a tourism domain, the page summary would contain information about tourist spots, contact numbers, animals, hotels, transport and more. Similarly a summary for a health domain may contain hospital info, medicine information, emergency contacts, symptoms of a disease and so on.

## CoRe Search Results and Analysis

A search engine based on CoRe framework was implemented by modifying the Nutch open source search engine. Over 50,000 documents in tourism domain were crawled and enconverted and indexed for search. An implementation of a Tamil keyword based search built with Nutch over the same set of documents and domain is taken for comparison.

### *Matrix Layout*

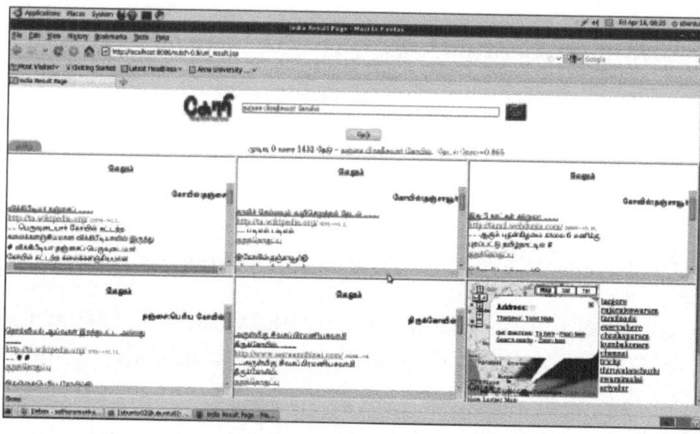

**Fig. 15.2: Matrix Layout**

In this chapter, we propose a Matrix Layout for displaying the results to the user. The Matrix Layout shown in figure 15.2, displays the results in a 3X2 matrix cells with each cell corresponding to a class of results based on the concepts and relationship between concepts. Figure 15.2 displays the results for the query தஞ்சை பிரகதீஸ்வரர் கோயில். (thanjai birakatheeswarar koayil) The first cell displays the results pertaining to the concepts that contain the actual keywords and sorted by the relation they have between them. Second cell identifies results that contain at least one concept with the actual keyword. The third cell identifies documents that will not be identified by traditional keyword search where none of the concepts contain keywords. In this case it retrieves documents with தஞ்சாவூர் & கோவில் (Thanjaavoor and Koavil) both of which do not form part of the actual query. The fourth and fifth cells are based on expansions of the query. Here they display results corresponding to பெரிய கோவில் & திருகோவில் Periya Koavil & Thirukkoavil). The final cell identifies the place associated with the query term to display the map of the corresponding place. The snapshot presented in Figure 15.2 is from our கோரி (CoRee) search engine implemented from the CoRe framework.

### *Performance Evaluation*

Precision of documents can be computed using the formula given below[8]. We compute the precision of documents for the first 5, first 10 and first 20 documents.

$$\text{precision} = \frac{[(\text{relevant document}) \cap (\text{retrieved documents})]}{[(\text{retrieved documents})]}$$

The average precision and mean average precision for a set of queries will indicate the performance of the system.

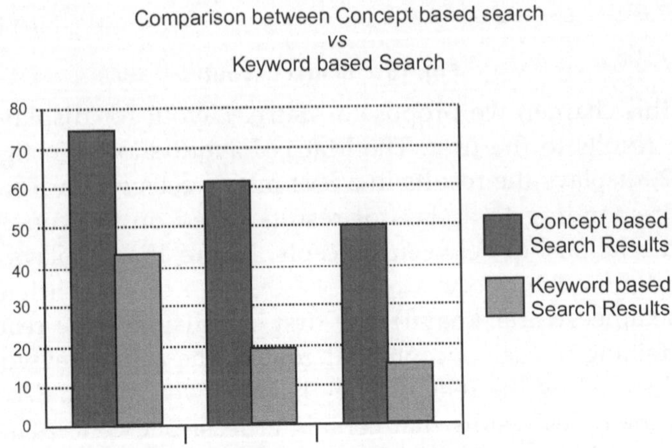


**Fig. 15.3 : Average Precision Comparison**

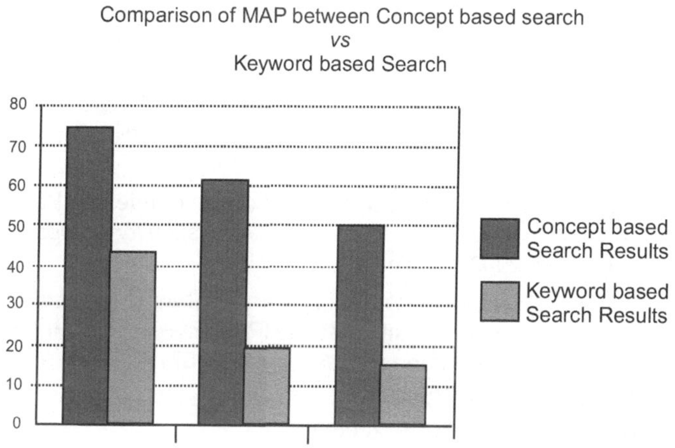


**Fig. 15.4 : Mean Average Precision Comparison**

For a set of 100 queries, precision is calculated at three levels for both the CoRe based search and keyword based search. The results are presented as a graph in figure 15.3. The mean average precision (MAP)[8] score comparison of the two search paradigms is given in figure 15.4.

## Conclusion and Future Work

This chapter describes CoRe, a framework for concept relation based search in Tamil. Different subsystems and components of the framework are described in detail. Results from an implementation of CoRe framework is provided and is compared against traditional keyword based search results. The rules of EnCoRe subsystem are very much domain specific. Expansion of the search engine to adapt to other domains will be future work. Integrating cross lingual results and providing cross lingual summary for the results will take this work to its next level.

## REFERENCES

1. Anandan, R. Parthasarathi, and Geetha, *Morphological Analyser for Tamil.* ICON 2002, 2002.

2. Chau, R. and C.-H. Yeh, *Fuzzy Conceptual Indexing for Concept-Based Cross-Lingual Text Retrieval*. IEEE Computer Society, 2004. 8(5).
3. Foundation, U., *The Universal Networking Language (UNL) Specifications* Version 3 3ed. December 2004: UNL Cente UNDL Foundation
4. Kang, B.-Y. A Novel Approach to Semantic Indexing Based on Concept. In *41st Annual Meeting on Association for Computational Linguistics* 2003. Japan.
5. Lacoste, C., et al., Inter-Media Concept-based Medical Image Indexing and Retrieval with UMLS at IPAL. *Evaluation of Multilingual and Multi-modal Information Retrieval*, 2007. 4730: p. 694-701.
6. Subalalitha, *et al.* CoReX : *A Concept Based Semantic Indexing Technique*. In SWM-08. 2008. India.
7. Surve, M., *et al.* AgroExplorer: a Meaning Based Multilingual Search Engine. *In International Conference on Digital Libraries*. 2004. Delhi, India: Sannella.
8. Andrew, T. and S. Falk. User Performance *versus* Precision Measures for Simple Search Tasks. *In 29th Annual international ACM SIGIR Conference on Research and Development in information Retrieval* 2006. Seattle, Washington, USA.

16

# Software Architectures for Tamil Mobile Learning

*— S. Swarnalatha*

**ABSTRACT**

*Our main objective in this chapter has been to extend the distribution of Tamil language learning materials and communication to lighter equipment, specifically PDA and mobile phone. The challenge is then to develop the system and server side to present materials in ways suitable for PDA technology, find acceptable solutions for distribution of materials and for administration to student, teacher to student/student to teacher and student to student communication. It is our aim in designing the environment for the mobile learner to extend and increase the flexibility of Tamil language education, that to some extent took a step backwards when converting from paper based to online learning, where students largely were required to study at a place (and at a time) where a computer with access the Internet was available.*

## Introduction

This chapter examines what kinds of software architecture might be used to build Mlearning systems and outlines what factors and issues should be considered in terms of the benefits and drawbacks of each generic architecture. In the following section we review some relevant literature on key aspects of m-Learning systems. We then outline a number of software architectures that may be used to build m-Learning applications, looking at how each approach may contribute to the requirements of m-Learning while considering the practical challenges and limitations. We provide a summary of the key issues associated with each architecture and suggest some recommendations for software architectures appropriate to different types of mobile learning system.

## Non-adaptive Mark-up

A number of mobile learning applications have been developed that use some specific form of browser mark-up for their client side presentation. This mark-up may be Wireless Markup Language (WML) or variations on the HyperText Markup Language (HTML) such as cHTML (compact HTML), XHTML (eXtensible HTML) Basic or XHTML Mobile Profile, depending on which types of mobile device are being supported. Regardless of the mark-up, the content may be served as static pages or generated dynamically on the server, using technologies such as server pages and/or e-Xtensible Stylesheet Language Transformations (XSLT) (Figure 16.1). Fowler classifies these to approaches to dynamic mark-up as the template (server page) and the transform (XSLT) approach, though in fact it is possible to combine the two, for example by using Tag libraries (such as the JSP standard tag library, the JSTL) in server pages that support transformations.

The advantage of this approach is that it is lightweight from the client device perspective requiring only the device's normal browser. The problem with non-adaptive mark-up is that using a particular mark-up language, for example WML, means that the content can only be rendered by browsers that understand that particular type of mark-up. Even though the content may be dynamically generated, it is only being generated for a specific type of client.

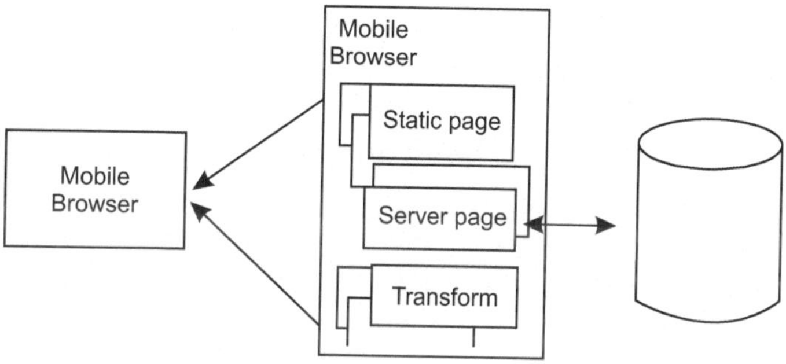


**Fig. 16.1: Non-adaptive mark-up architecture**

## Adaptive Mark-Up

Adaptive mark-up requires a server side process that is able to generate mark-up appropriate to the mobile device from a common set of contents. There are a number of approaches to this, for example an application can interrogate the HTTP (HyperText Transfer Protocol) header of the request and identify the client browser type from the 'user-agent' field, then generate client specific mark-up using various XSL transformations. An alternative approach is to use a tag library

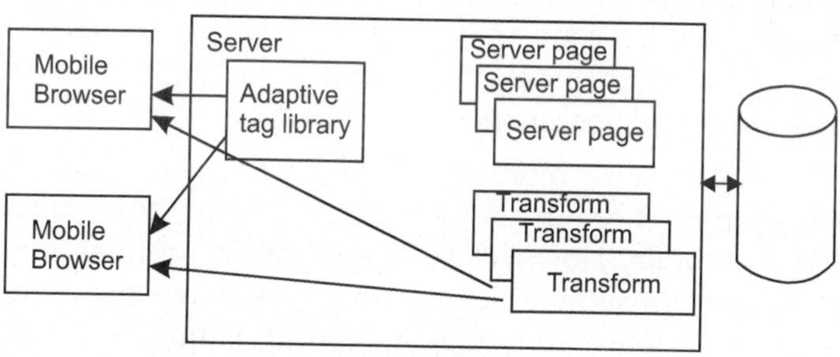


**Fig. 16.2: Adaptive mark-up architecture**

such as Wireless Abstraction Library (WALL), a JSP tag library that builds on the Wireless Universal Resource File (WURFL). WURFL is able to recognise user agent information and identify different devices, while WALL generates device specific mark-up. Either way, the advantage of this approach is that it enables a Mlearning application to support multiple types of mobile browser (Figure 16.2).

### *Mobile Client Side Application*

While the mark-up approach to m-Learning architectures can provide a good range of content across a wide range of devices, confining the learner's activity to what can be supported by a mobile browser can limit the range of learning activities that are possible on the device. For example, interactive learning games may be difficult or impossible to support. An alternative approach to using mark-up to provide content via the mobile Internet is to provide applications that can be downloaded to the mobile device. There are three general categories of application that may be developed for mobile devices.

The first approach is an application written for a specific mobile device platform, for example targeting a particular model or make of mobile phone. These applications can take advantage of the special characteristics of that particular device, which can make them, for example, highly per formant, but of course these applications cannot be used on other devices. A second approach is to use Microsoft Windows based applications, for example building an application using Windows Mobile components.

This approach is more generic than writing for a particular device, since there are a number of devices that support Widows Mobile. However such applications cannot run on the majority of mobile devices, since there are many other operating systems being used including Palm OS, Symbian and Linux. The third, most generic approach, is to use Java Micro Edition (Java ME)ý. Using this software platform enables us to deliver a relatively rich client experience to a wide range of devices. Although Java ME has its limitations compared to some other application platforms such as Symbian and BREW, it works across a large proportion of mobile devices, including many Windows phones. In the context of mobile phones, the specific configuration and profile typically installed is the Connected Limited Device Configuration (CLDC) supporting the Mobile Information Device Profile (MIDP).

Java ME applications that run using this profile are known as MIDlets. Of course coding at the higher level of abstraction that enables interoperability has its costs in performance terms. For example Java ME applications have been shown to execute at about half the speed of equivalent C programs. There are also issues regarding the version of both the CLDC and MIDlet specifications that a given phone may support. Important differences between versions include floating point number support and security management, among many others. If a mobile client application is chosen as the software architecture, then the overall system design is simple.

The application runs standalone on the client, so the only role of the server is to enable download and installation of the application (Figure 16.3). This may be done either wirelessly or using a cable. Wireless download of Java applications can be provided using OTA (over the air) provisioning, a standardized approach that provides a consistent client-server interaction and enables version control for application

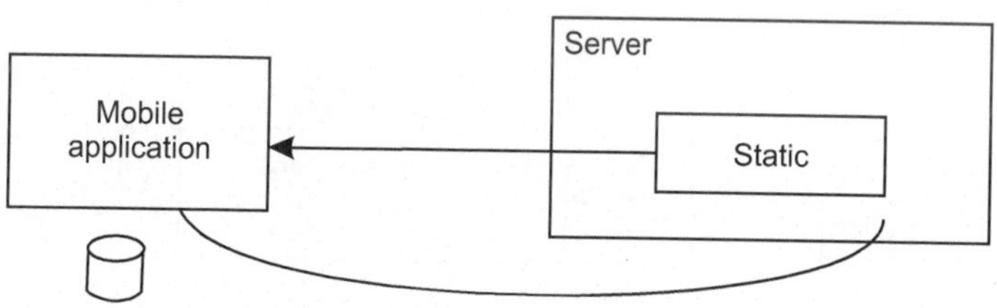


**Fig. 16.3: Client side application architecture**

downloads. The mobile application may use the data store on the mobile device but will not require access to any server side resources.

## Smart Client with Server Connectivity

So far we have considered two very different types of software architectures for mobile learning systems; one based on providing a page based mobile Internet system, the other using a downloadable application client. However there is another approach that combines features from both of these architectures, the smart client that connects to the server. In this approach, there is a client side application, but that application does not run standalone. Rather, it communicates with the server to send and receive information while the application is running (Figure 16.4). There are a number of advantages to this approach. First, it is possible for the mobile learning application to provide a much wider set of content than is possible with a single downloaded application, since the storage size of the mobile device limits the amount of learning content that can be downloaded. A smart client that connects to the server can access learning content on demand without having to keep it all stored in the mobile device. Similarly, we can utilise the server to store information about the clients so we can, for example, maintain a sophisticated user profile on the server. In addition, the ability of the device to communicate data with the server in both directions (upload

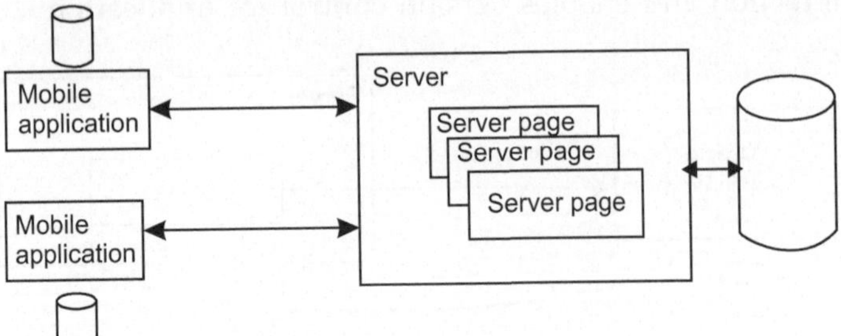


**Fig. 16.4: Smart client with server connectivity architecture**

and download) means that it is possible to build a collaborative learning system where multiple users can send and receive data to and from each other.

The price we must pay for this power and flexibility is complexity. For example, data management becomes a more complex issue because there may be data stored in a local data store on the client device as well as on the server. Mobile databases will need to be synchronized with central databases, and cache management has to be sophisticated to cope with the small memory size in most mobile devices.

Distributed smart client applications using this architecture also need an appropriate communication protocol, such as XML over HTTP, to enable the client to access server side resources at run time. Tamil Language Learning through Mobile m-Learning offers a powerful and practical solution to many learning and training challenges, such as:

- in collaborative projects and fieldwork
- as a classroom alternative to books or computers
- where learners are widely dispersed
- to engage with learners who in the past have felt excluded
- in promotional and awareness campaigns
- for 'just-in-time' employee training.

From a teaching and learning point of view, campus-wide internet access - or even access that targets social and learning spaces such as refectories, libraries, lecture rooms and labs – is what truly blends together online and face-to-face learning. It means that while they're on campus, a student can access their online learning just by turning on their net book or iPhone. They can contribute to class online discussions while eating lunch or access their readings before class, using the technology they already have with them: their laptop, net book, or other wi-fi capable mobile device.

For mobile language learning—and even for flexible learning - at any educational institution, equipping formal and informal learning spaces (such as social spaces) with fundamental enabling technologies like wireless internet access has to be at the top of the priority list. It even makes sense from a budget point of view, as every laptop a student brings in and uses takes pressure off the student labs. This, in turn, reduces the amount that has to be spent on standard-image, admin-locked, physical lab computers... and frees students to use their own computers which can be configured to best support their particular program of study.

## Conclusion

In this chapter we have provided a brief overview of four software architectures for mobile learning; non adaptive mark-up, adaptive mark-up, mobile client side application and smart client with server connectivity. All of these architectures have their own strengths and weaknesses, and in most cases we are trading flexibility against complexity. In addition there are different levels of server connectivity required for these different architectures, and successful applications depend not only on the technical infrastructure but also the social context within which issues such as pricing come into play. Therefore deciding on suitable software architecture for a specific m-Learning system depends not only on technical factors but also an analysis of the user context. While we may see that smart client architecture with server connectivity can provide us with the richest mobile learning environment, alternative architectures may prove easier to install, more robust in use, more easily deployed to a larger range of devices and cheaper for the learner to maintain. Therefore the most important aspect of designing an m-Learning system architecture is to consider all aspects of the user context rather than just focus on the technical platform.

## REFERENCES


1. The Use of Palmtop Computers for Learning—A Review of the Literature—Learning and Skills Development Agency.
2. The Use of Computer and Video Games for Learning—Alice Mitchell & Carol Savill-Smith.
3. http://www.xenglobaltech.com/j2me-mobile-applications.html
4. http://www.nextwavemultimedia.com/html/mobilegaming.html http://learning.ericsson.net/mlearning2/project_one/wap_article.html
5. Software Architectures for Mobile Learning D. Parsons & H. Ryu Chang, C. and J. Sheu (2002). Design and Implementation of Ad hoc Classroom and Eschoolbag Systems for Ubiquitous Learning. IEEE Int. Workshop Wireless and Mobile Technologies in Education.
6. Chen, Y., T. Kao, *et al.* (2002). A Mobile Scaffolding-aid-based Bird-watching Learning Systems. IEEE Int. Workshop Wireless and Mobile Technologies in Education. Coulton, P., O. Rashid, *et al.* (2005). "Creating Entertainment Applications for Cellular Phones." ACM Computers in Entertainment 3(3).
7. Domer, J., M. Nanja, et al. (2004). Comparative Performance Analysis of Mobile Runtimes on Intel XScale® Technology. 2004 Workshop on Interpreters, Virtual Machines and Emulators (IVME'04), Washington, D.C., USA, ACM Press.

17

# Predictive Tamil Short Messages for Handheld Devices

—*Abirami, S., Vilvanathan, K. and Baskaran, R.*


### ABSTRACT

*This chapter aims at providing ease and flexibility to Tamil SMS users by suggesting the commonly used message templates with few key strokes, based on the context of letter typed. This system intends to predict short messages in Tamil, as similar to T9 dictionary, but the scope is not restricted to the prediction of a single word. Rather this attempt to predict the short messages (sentences) communicated in our day-to-day life.*

*Initially, keypad of the mobile phone has been configured with Tamil Vowels and Consonants using Tamil keypad layout standardized for hand held devices. To start with, this predictive SMS system allows the user to type an initial letter in Tamil to predict the possible nouns and verbs starting with the letter typed. Based on the user selection, initial word gets composed. If the initial word appears to be a noun, probable actions (i.e. Verbs) associated with the noun with proper case endings could be predicted. Depending on the needs of the user, verbal actions could be enriched with suitable adverbs too. If the initial word appears to be an adverb, suitable verb could be appended with it.*

*Possible templates (nouns, verbs and adverbs) are stored in Unicode text format in a file (records). Depending on the context (taking nouns, case markers and adverbs into account), suitable records would be retrieved. Few English message templates are available in standard mobile phones to reduce the typing hindrance involved in messaging. Moreover, these templates are not applicable to Tamil language. As a result, this chapter has been motivated to introduce a Predictive SMS system which intends to reduce the number of key presses required to frame a message in Tamil. In addition, this system covers most of the commonly used Tamil sentences and not restricted to fewer templates, thereby attempting to provide a full fledged predictive Tamil short message service.*

## Introduction

Now-a-days, SMS through mobile phones have become an integral part of human communication. To make it easier and innovative, it is important to have the facility to enter, send, receive and read SMS's in Tamil. SMS in Tamil are already a reality. This chapter is therefore, we believe, the first attempt to come out with a possibility to send SMS's in Tamil, as comfortably as one sends an SMS in English. To add flavour to it, we try to make it more easily than English.

## Tamil language

Tamil is a South Indian language spoken widely in Tamil Nadu in India. Tamil has the longest unbroken literary tradition amongst the Dravidian languages. The earliest available text is the Tolkaapiyam, a work describing the language of the classical period. There are several other famous works in Tamil like Kambar Ramayanam and Silapathigaram but few supports in Tamil which speaks about the greatness of the language. For example the Thirukural is translated into most other languages due to its richness in content. It is a collection of two sentence poems efficiently conveying and few other things in a hidden language called Slaydai in Tamil. Tamil has 12 vowels and 18 consonants. These are combined with each other to yield 216 composite characters and 1 special character (aayatha ezhuthu) counting to a total of (12+18+216+1) 247 characters.

### Vowels

Vowels in Tamil are otherwise called UyirEzhuthu and are of two types short (Kuril) and long (Nedil).

### Consonants

Consonants are classified into three classes with 6 in each class and are called Vallinam, Idaiyinam, and Mellinam.

### Tamil Unicode

The Unicode Standard (http://www.unicode.org) is the Universal Character encoding scheme for written characters and text. It defines the uniform way of encoding multilingual text that enables the exchange of text data internationally and creates the foundation of global software. The Tamil Unicode range is U+0B80 to U+0BFF. The Unicode characters are comprised of 2 bytes in nature. For example, the Unicode for the character is அ 0B85; the Unicode for the character மீ is 0BAE+0BC0. The Unicode is designed for various other Tamil characters.

## Functional Block Diagram

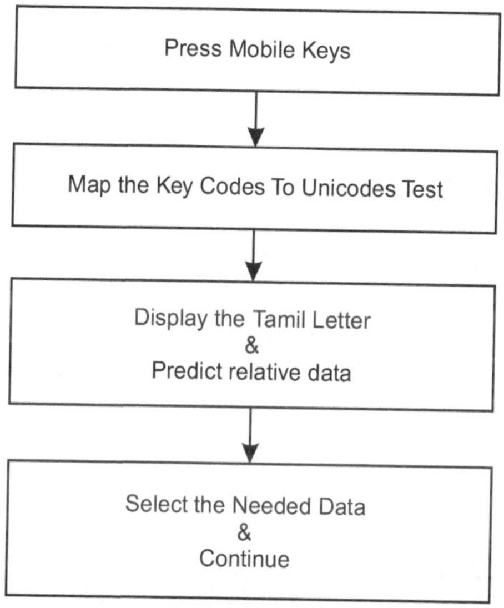


## Taking Key Codes as Input

When the user presses the keys of the mobile phone, the key press event generates unique key codes for each key. Using those keys codes and the time interval between key press events, the appropriate Tamil letter is mapped and displayed on the screen.

## Keyboard Mapping

Mobile Phone Keyboards have a limited number of keys (roughly 12). However, the use of the mobile phone as a messaging instrument (using SMS) has risen in the recent past. Currently, predictive texting schemes exist for English and many European and other languages. However, such a scheme does not exist for most Indian languages, including Tamil. Moreover, the mobile phone keyboard for the English Language is generally arranged in the alphabetical order, that is the key for the number 2 contains the letters A,B,C; that for number 3 contains D, E, F; and so on. Following a similar arrangement is a relatively inefficient scheme for Tamil; hence, we have come out with a more efficient arrangement that does not club frequently used letters on the same key. Our mapping assigns, in general, two vowel and two consonants to each key.

While pressing a key, the first letter assigned to that key is mapped. If the same key is pressed again, the time between the subsequent key strokes are calculated. If the time is below the quantum time assigned, instead of the first letter, the second letter assigned to that key is mapped. The same concept is applied for all the letters assigned to the keys. When a consonant letter is pressed and subsequently if a vowel is keyed in, its corresponding consonant letter is mapped. For example, ma+e=mi.

## Stored Records

The Possible Sentences used often are stored in the records, as far now, it is limited so as to make the work easier. The sentences are stored in Unicode format, thus making the size of records minimal.

## Predict

As the keys are pressed and the corresponding Tamil characters are displayed in the screen, the system searches for the matching sentences in the Records and if any matches, they are displayed as choices. When the first letter is typed, the system searches for sentences starting with that letter in the record. And displays the possible sentences, the user can select one from that choice or can go for a different choice of typing in the second letter. Now the records are searched for sentences starting with that two letters combined. And the possible sentences are displayed. Now the user can select one from that choice or can go on for typing in the next letter. The same procedure follows for every letter typed.

## Future work

This chapter limits the sentences in Records to a meaningful limit, we can increase the records in future for a better system. The user interface is also restricted to our convenience, it can be changed to a standard format.

## Conclusion

This system encompasses the Tamil typing and prediction of the sentences as and when typing. This eliminates the typing and time to a considerable extent. Also it helps a person with less knowledge in Tamil typing and spelling.

# 18

# Status of Unicode in the Indian Tamil Publishing Industry

—P. Chellappan

The publishing industry in general including the Tamil Publishing industry is at a crucial juncture today. The world of publishing is moving away slowly but surely from the traditional paper based publication towards e-Book publication. This movement is more significant in English books than Tamil books. Nevertheless the Tamil publishing industry has to gear itself as soon as possible, so as not to fall behind and get lost in the technological revolution. The Tamil Publishing industry has traditionally been using 8 bit encodings just like all the other Indian languages. But looking at the future, it has to move over to 16 bit encodings. The purpose of this study is to ascertain the current practices in the Tamil publishing industry so that suitable steps can be taken to help in this transition.

## Methodology

A questionnaire was prepared and distributed to some of the

major Tamil books, and newspaper publishers. The questionnaire mainly relates to the pre-press activities such as receipt of manuscripts, data entry, page layout, and graphic designing. The feedback was then analyzed.

## Summary of analysis

In all 30 Book Publishers and 10 Magazine and Newspaper publishers were asked for their feedback. But only 11 responses were received from Book Publishers and 9 were received from Magazine and Newspaper publishers. It can be safely assumed that there will not be a significant difference in the findings even if the remaining feed back was received. The data was analyzed and statistics are presented in the tables given below. In these tables (B P) refers to Book Publishers and (M & N) refers to Magazines and Newspapers.

**Receipt of Manuscripts**

| | Hard Copy | Soft Copy |
|---|---|---|
| BP | 84.00% | 16.00% |
| M&N | 4.00% | 96.00% |

| | Tam | TSCII | Unicode | Others |
|---|---|---|---|---|
| BP | 44.00% | 12.00% | 19.00% | 25.00% |
| M&N | 67.00% | — | — | 33.00% |

It can clearly be seen that in the BP segment manuscripts are received mostly as either hand written or typed documents. But in the M&N segment it is quite the opposite. 96 per cent of the manuscripts are received as soft copies. These soft copies are again received in various font encodings. Fortunately, in most cases a single manuscript comes in a single encoding. So encoding conversion operations are reduced to a minimum, unless of course it is absolutely essential like in the case of manuscripts received in Unicode.

Type Setting:

| | In-house | Outsourced |
|---|---|---|
| BP | 23.00% | 77.00% |
| M&N | 100.00% | 0.00% |

| | Tam | TSCII | Unicode | Others |
|---|---|---|---|---|
| BP | 44.00% | 12.00% | 19.00% | 25.00% |
| M&N | 67.00% | — | — | 33.00% |

| | Page Maker | Indesign | Quark | Others |
|---|---|---|---|---|
| BP | 57.00% | 10.00% | 25.00% | 25.00% |
| M&N | 10.00% | 20.00% | 10.00% | 60.00% |

Type Setting operation is one of the first major operations done by any publisher. Most of them have only limited in-house capability and the rest is outsourced. As can be seen in the tables above, the BP segment has 23 per cent in-house capability but the M&N segment has 100 per cent in-house capability. The major advantage of having in-house capability is in the tight control over font usage. In the case of outsourced operations, the publishers have little control over the font encoding used. Some times they are even forced to accept documents that use different font encoding since the DTP operator has only that option. Some of the publishers are either ignorant or do not even bother about the font encodings, as they archive the books only as hard copies.

## Page Layout

| | In-house | Outsourced |
|---|---|---|
| BP | 27.00% | 73.00% |
| M&N | 100.00% | 0.00% |

| | Tam | TSCII | Unicode | Others |
|---|---|---|---|---|
| BP | 50.00% | 14.00% | — | 30.00% |
| M&N | 67.00% | — | — | 33.00% |

| | Page Maker | Indesign | Quark | Others |
|---|---|---|---|---|
| BP | 52.00% | 23.00% | 10.00% | 1.500% |
| M&N | 11.00% | 78.00% | 11.00% | — |

Page Layout is an important aspect in the publication of any book, magazine or newspaper. It can be seen that in the BP segment 73 per cent of this operation is outsourced. The reason is that they would like to leave it to the professionals. However in the M&N segment 100 per cent of the page layout is done in-house.

Newspapers and magazines have very little time on hand before the matter goes to print. Hence it makes sense to do this important job in-house. One important aspect here is that UNICODE is not used in this final stage. This is attributable to the applications used for page layout. Page Maker, Indesign and Quark do not support complex script and hence cannot be used for Tamil, or for that matter any Indian language.

## Graphic Design

| | In-house | Outsourced |
|---|---|---|
| BP | 34.00% | 66.00% |
| M&N | 100.00% | 0.00% |

| | Tam | TSCII | Unicode | Others |
|---|---|---|---|---|
| BP | 54.00% | 7.00% | — | 39.00% |
| M&N | 67.00% | — | — | 33.00% |

| | Photoshop | Illustrator | Corel Draw | Others |
|---|---|---|---|---|
| BP | 57.00% | 10.00% | 25.00% | 25.00% |
| M&N | 33.00% | 33.00% | 33.00% | — |

All the observations for Page Layout are exactly applicable for Graphic Design also. Here also the applications used viz.

Photoshop, Illustrator and CorelDraw do not support complex script rendering. Hence Unicode encoded text cannot be used in this step.

## Conclusion

The survey clearly indicates that the entire publishing industry uses only 8 bit encoded fonts like TAM and TSCII, with TAM being used more widely than the other encodings. It also indicates that even when the original manuscript is received in Unicode; it is being converted into one of the 8 bit encodings for further use. This is mainly due to lack of support of complex script rendering in the applications that are used in the publishing industry. The lack of awareness of UNICODE amongst the book publishers is also another contributing factor for non-usage of UNICODE. The reason for this lack of awareness can also be attributed to the non-usability of this encoding.

However all the publishers in the M&N segment are aware of UNICODE and in fact about 55% of the publishers in the M&N segment use UNICODE for their on-line editions? They refrain from using UNICODE in the print editions only due to the lack of support for complex script rendering in the applications that are used by them.

In the coming days when use of multiple languages in a single publication becomes more common, it is better to migrate from the legacy 8 bit encodings to 16 bit encodings. The inhibiting factor as already stated above is the lack of support for complex script rendering. Since a definite time frame is not available for provision of this support, usage of an all character 16 bit encoding like TACE16 will help in immediate migration to the 16 bit environment. One additional advantage of TACE is that even off-theshelf e-Book readers will be able to render Tamil e-Books embedded with a TACE font.

19

# Problems of Using Unicode in Software Components and in NLP

— *Dr. V. Krishnamoorthy*

***ABSTRACT***

*To speed up software development and reduce cost, using specialised software components is an established practice. Tamil editing software developers have been using a component called 'text control', to include functionalities like justification and tables. These components do not support complex scripts. Hence they are not usable for using Unicode Tamil in the software. It is not known when such support will be provided. Economic considerations may indicate that it may not come through in the immediate future. The processing of letters, words, sentences, paragraphs and passages to 'understand' what they mean, and, produce answers to the required questions is the basic aim of Natural Language Processing (NLP). This has string processing as the core. The encoding of Tamil in Unicode is not very conducive to this string processing is shown by taking a few simple fundamental operations. The complex behaviour is the result of the variable length encoding and unnatural way of representation of letters in Unicode.*

## Introduction

It is now widely known that Unicode Tamil is not supported in high-end publishing software. But less known is the fact that some software components also do not support Unicode Tamil. This may pose restrictions on developing specialised Tamil software in the long run. Here we highlight this problem by giving a specific example. We find that the reason for not supporting Unicode Tamil is that Tamil in Unicode needs level 2 implementation.

There are many special editing software for Tamil, which provide many other special features not available in Word etc. All these software use software components called 'Text control'. This text control component is essential to provide the functionalities like, justification and tables. It is not possible to create such components on our own, for our own use, in view of the complexity involved. Tamil software developers, like many other developers world wide, use these components, to provide rich functionalities within their software. When Unicode is used in these components, the following problems arise. Complex script support is not available in text controls, which are available today. Absence of this leads to incorrect alignment and undesirable and unacceptable editing experience. As such these components cannot be used for Tamil Unicode. The component developers are not willing to specify when they will provide support for complex scripts. It is seen that these components work with the Tamil All Character Encoding (TACE). In the second part, the differences in dealing with the current Unicode and the all character encoding, in the context of natural language processing is brought out. Specifically how the fundamental operations are done easily and quickly in the all character encoding is studied. This shows that keeping the data in the all character encoding will speed up the NLP in Tamil.

## Using Tamil Unicode in Components

Software components called Text Controls are used in many

Bilingual text editors. Currently they do not provide full support for Tamil. They open the file with Tamil Unicode characters. But the visible cursor position does not correspond to the 'actual' cursor position. If one tries to insert a letter or string at a particular position, especially near the end of a line, it gets inserted somewhere else. An example is shown in Figure 19.1.

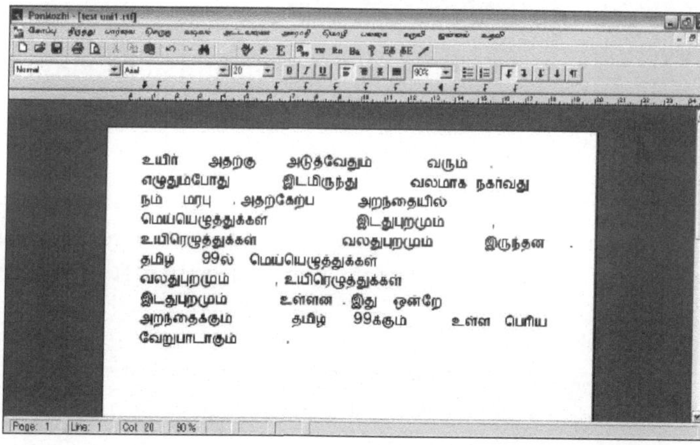


**Fig. 19.1.**

Here the cursor is placed at the end of the third word in the first line, which is 'aduththum', and the letter 'vee' is inserted using the 'paste' operation. The letter gets inserted in the middle of the third word. It seems that this is due to the wrong calculation of the width of the letters. Here it seems that the letters are treated as having constant width. This can be seen by keeping the cursor at the left and tapping the right arrow key repeatedly. Also if 'select all' is given, the selected portion is shown wrongly. See Figure 19.2 for the left aligned text. The mismatch is clearly visible. Similar mismatch is seen in the case of the justified text also. It is obvious that no commercial software can be sold with such grave shortcomings.

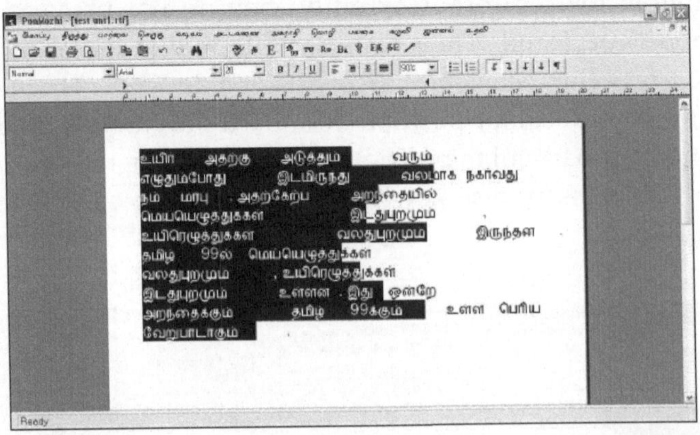

Fig. 19.2.

Figure 19.3 shows that the text and the selected area match correctly in the case of text in all character encoding. The widths are correctly calculated and the insertion is done correctly.

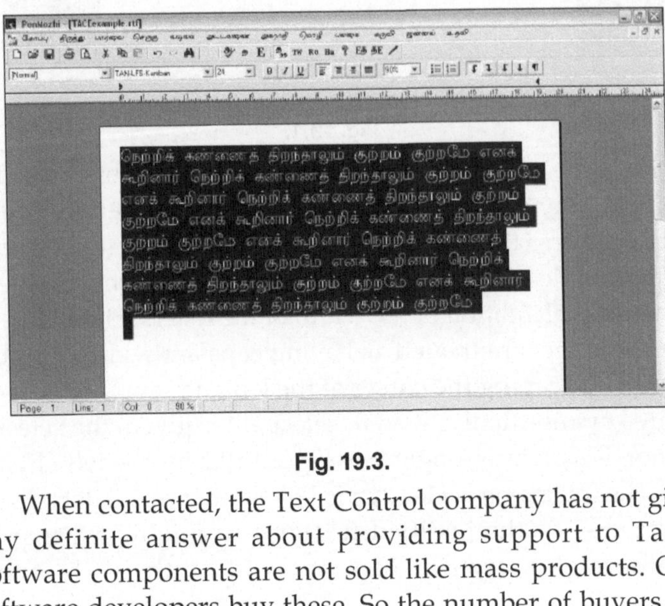

Fig. 19.3.

When contacted, the Text Control company has not given any definite answer about providing support to Tamil. Software components are not sold like mass products. Only software developers buy these. So the number of buyers will not be very large. When it comes to a particular language, this number may be very small. This may discourage many of these component vendors, who are not big companies, from providing support for a complex script, since it my involve considerable cost. This indicates that no Tamil application using Tamil Unicode can make use of many good components in the near future. Whereas most of them may work without any difficulty with the all character encoding.

## Problems in NLP

Comparing two strings is a fundamental operation, used heavily in NLP. For example, when a new word has to be added to an existing dictionary, the new word has to be put in the proper place. Otherwise it will lead to linear search, which is time consuming. When we compare two strings, it is natural to expect that the natural ordering of letters in Tamil be followed. This is essential, as the sorted sequence of words may be required to be printed for the human perusal, or stored for use in some other application.

Comparing two Tamil strings in Unicode is a formidable task, since the ordering of characters in Unicode does not follow the Tamil ordering. Also, the letters ksha and sri, which we consider as single letters, are stored as a combination of two or more characters. In the all character encoding, this task is just as easy as saying 1,2,3. The pseudo code for this can be given below:

```
Let minLength = minimum (length (string1), length
(string2) )
For I = 0 to minLength-1
If (string1[I] > string2[I]) then string1 is bigger. Exit
// here the common part is same.
If ( length(string1) > length(string2) )
then string1 is bigger.
else string2 is bigger.
```

### *Exit*

Writing the pseudo code in the case of Unicode is not so easy. I do not attempt it here, due to lack of patience on my part. But, note that the following things have to be taken care of while comparing.

- The consonants with 'a', have to be rearranged according to Tamil sorting order.
- The mei pulli should come before any of the vowel mathras.
- A consonant with 'a', with the pulli coming next to it, precedes that consonant with 'a'.
- Ksha series letters should not be put in the ka series, though the first character is ka.
- Sri has to be put in a separate place. The length of the string is not the same as the number of letters. String length cannot be used straightaway.
- One may understand the complexity and the time involved in writing this code. The time involved in executing these two codes is obvious.

### *Let us take another simple example*

Hyphenation is a problem faced in the printing industry. Let us consider a simple solution for this, with the following rules. Break only when there are 4 or more letters. At least 2 letters should on both sides of the cutting point. The second part should not start with a pure consonant. (This solution has been implemented by us already.)

In the case of all character encoding, the pseudo code would look like this.

If ( lenth ( word ) < 4 ) exit.

// length is 4 or more, here

// try to accommodate as much as possible in the first line

for I = length(word) -2 to 2 do

if word[I+1] is not a consonant, and, first I letters fit in the first line,

then split after the I-th letter. Exit.

Considering the same solution in Unicode, the following things need attention.

The length of the string does not give the number of letters. Hence the condition that at least two letters on both sides has to be taken care of separately. The boundary points of the 'for loop' does not ensure this.

The cutting may happen at the middle of the letter. So every time it should be assured that we do not cut at the middle of a letter. Special attention is needed for sri and ksha series letters.

All these will need more coding and more execution time.

We will close with one more examples.

Searching for a string as it is, has limited scope in Tamil. In Tamil, words appear with many variations.

For example the word 'maram' appears as 'maraththil', 'maramaaka' etc. To find out all the places in which 'maram' appears, it has to locate all the words with variations also. A simple solution will be to first search for the string 'mara', and then find out whether the word found is a required word. For this start checking whether the next letter is 'im' or 'th'.

The same logic works for both Unicode and TACE. But the difference is the number of false hits. In Unicode, when 'mara' is searched, all the words with 'mar', 'mara', 'maraa', mari', ... will be the results of the search. This will result in a large set which has to be filtered for the required words. But in the case of TACE, only words having 'mara' will be found out. Others will not appear in the searched words. This will save the time for processing the unwanted words to a great extent.

In the three simple examples provided, we have shown that in the case of Unicode, the coding may be complicated, and even when the coding may be the same, some unnecessary work may be done. In view of the above, we can conclude that the processing for NLP will be easier and faster, and the running time will be less when TACE is used, when compared with Unicode. Also the internal data, like dictionary, kept in TACE will make the processing easier and quicker.

## Conclusion

It is shown that some useful software components, which are being used by Tamil editing software developers, do not support Tamil Unicode. The complexity of executing fundamental operations of NLP using Unicode is brought out. These are due to the level 2 implementation of Tamil in Unicode, and, the variable and unnatural way the encoding is done. It is shown that the all character encoding provides a simple natural way of encoding, and hence provides better results.

## REFERENCES

1. Unicode.org
2. www.tamilvu.org/coresite/download/TACE16_Report_English.pdf

# 20

# Challenges of Publishing Industry and e-Governance with Tamil Unicode (TU) and Possible Remedies with Tamil All Character Encoding in 16-bit (TACE16)

—*A. Elangovan*

## Introduction

India is emerging as the Publishing hub of the world with 45 per cent of publications in English, the world's third largest English publishing country after UK and USA. The remaining 55 per cent is published in Indian languages. Today Print media is still the largest media in terms of readership, circulation, published pages and editorial manpower involved. Today publishing does not stop with print media but also extends to web, mobile, palm readers and broadcast media.

e-Governance in India is in its nascent stage. Indian language enabling is essential for the successful implementation of any e-Governance project. e-Governance will include all media including web, print, mobile and palm readers. The data should be viewable, portable and reliable across various media, operating systems and applications. Multilingual publishing is still a major challenge for publishers in spite of the Unicode advantage of having all languages of the world under one unified encoding scheme.

Today most of the content available in the web is in Unicode and Tamil Unicode is widely used by all segments of people. Inspite of its popularity, the Publishing Industry and e-Governance segment face several challenges in implementing Tamil Unicode. This paper explains the specific areas of challenges and the possible remedial measures to some of them. It also forewarns the users about the pit falls in the implementation of Tamil Unicode and how to avoid them. The paper discusses some of the implementation issues faced in real life projects with Tamil Unicode and the remedial measures taken. The paper also covers some possible solutions which include Innovative methods of Unicode Font design, TACE16 based applications and Software Plug-in Tools and its benefits.

## Challenges in Publishing with Tamil Unicode

### *Text Editing*

Today the editors have a wide choice of sources for the news, stories, events and statistical data. The sources include wire services, news agencies, reporters, journalists including freelancers, web sites, blogs, TV channels, digital archives and printed archives. The text data exchange mostly happens in the digital form through email and in other formats like pure text, word, spread sheet and PDF. More and more content in Tamil Unicode (TU) is available in the web, email and word formats and is becoming a popular source of information. However the text need to be converted to 8-bit legacy encoding like TAB/TAM before it can be paginated as most of the publishing applications like Adobe, Quark and Corel do not support TU yet. Converters are widely available to convert TU in pure text format and the availability for other formats like word is limited. We face two problems while doing this conversion. First, if the TU text contains more than one language *i.e.* Tamil and English, the text in English gets converted to junk. This requires manual intervention to identify the English text, apply the English font, proof read the text and correct all junk characters before they are sent to pagination. The second one being loss of all formatting done in other applications like word while doing this conversion. The typical text process flow is given in (Fig. 20.1).

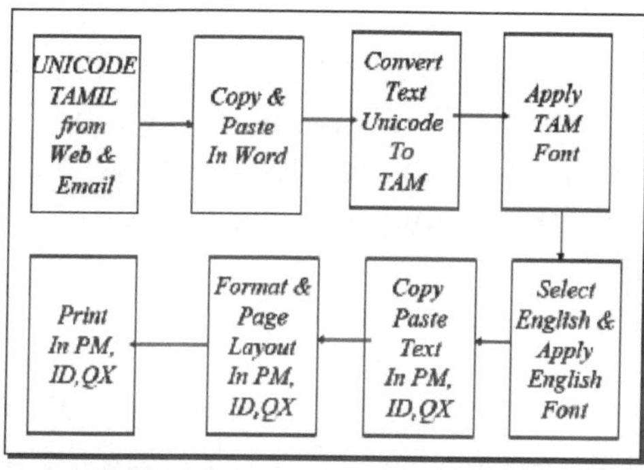


**Fig. 20.1: TU Text Editing Process Flow**

**Solutions:** One way to overcome the problem of multi-lingual text is to convert Unicode text to TACE16 (Tamil All Character Encoding for 16 bit) instead of 8-bit TAB/TAM. TACE16 can easily coexist with other language text in Unicode. It is possible to retain the formatting features of the source document with help of plug-ins for conversion from within the respective applications. E.g. Indesign Encoding Converter plug-in.

## *Pagination*

MS Word and Publisher are used to some extent in the entry level and do support Tamil Unicode with some limitations. PageMaker has been discontinued by Adobe few years back and anyway it does not support 16-bit encoding like Unicode. The most widely used pagination applications by professional publishers like Newspapers, Magazines, Books, Directories, Government publications like budget documents, gazette publications, assembly documents are Adobe Indesign, Quark

Xpress and Corel Draw. Unfortunately all these professional applications which are vital for publishing and printing are yet to provide TU support even in their latest versions (Fig. 20.2A). And the definite date of their future support is also not yet known. Also about 30% of the publishing industry uses Apple Macintosh systems, where the TU support is incomplete.

***Solutions***: Interestingly TACE16, which is the standard recommended by TN Task Force is found to be working well in all the above professional applications (Fig 20.2B). It is also supported both in Windows and MacOSX operating systems. Real life trials in production have proved not only its support but also its higher efficiency.

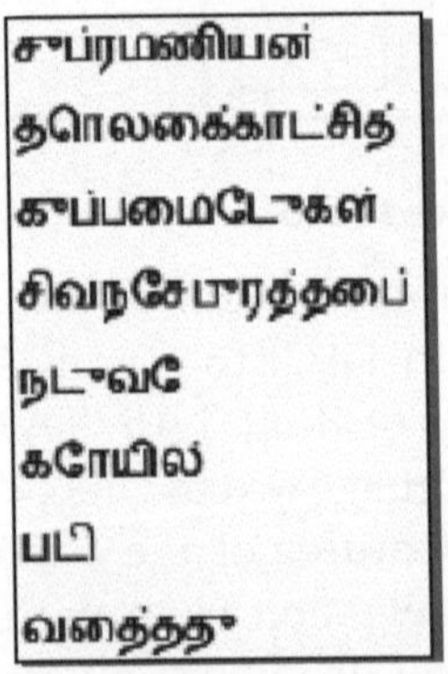

**Fig. 20.2A: TU in Indesign and Quark**

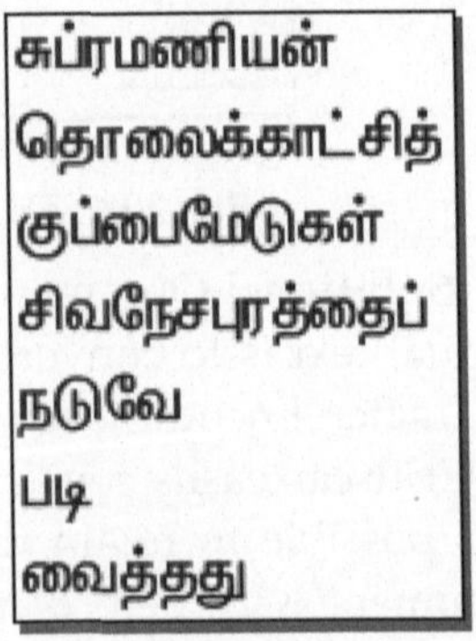


**Fig. 20.2B: TACE16 in Indesign and Quark**

### *Illustrations*

Graphic illustrations like logos, graphs, charts, cartoons, sketches, back grounds, banners and book illustrations form important elements of publishing for not only print but also for web and mobile. The popular applications used for creating graphic illustrations are Adobe Illustrator and Corel Draw. Unfortunately both of them are yet to provide TU support. (Fig. 20.3A and 20.3B)

Fig. 20.3A: TU in Corel Draw

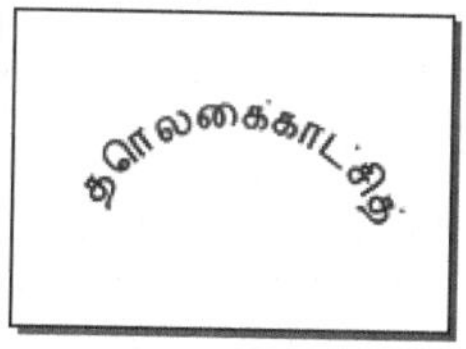

Fig. 20.3B: TU in Adobe Iluustrator

Fig. 20.3C: TACE16 in TACE16

*Solutions*: Fortunately TACE16 is found to be working well in both these applications in both Windows and MacOSX. (Fig. 20.3C)

## Image Editing

Photo editing, painting, colour correction, titling and labeling images are the next important functions of publishing. The leading application for image editing for print, web and animation is Adobe Photoshop. Corel Photo Paint is also used to some extent. Both these packages are yet to provide TU support.

*Solutions*: Once again TACE16 is found to be working well in both these applications in both Windows and MacOSX.

## PDF Data Storage

Adobe PDF, the most popular Portable Document Format is almost the de-facto standard in print and publishing for creating the print ready format. PDF provides the portability of printing the documents across any printing device irrespective of the application and operating system in which it was originally created. It provides option for embedding the original fonts making it possible to print in any device without the need for having the original fonts at the printing end. PDF made it possible to electronically transfer print ready document across the world, paving the way for phenomenal growth of the growth of the e-Publishing (Electronic Publishing) industry. PDF is also the most popular format for storage of documents both for short term and long term. PDF retains the original text and graphics, which can be extracted and edited for future use. ISO standards for PDF are well defined and extensively used by the print and publishing industry while defining specifications and printing standards. Adobe PDF does not provide support for the complex rendering process in Tamil Unicode. The Unicode text is stored inside PDF in its own native format, different from that of the Unicode rendering order. When the Tamil Unicode text is extracted from the stored PDF documents, and placed back into MS Word, some characters with Egara, Eegera, Ugara, Uugara and Augara modifiers get reordered and sometimes even joins with the previous consonants, making the text meaningless (Fig. 20.4A).

| Unicode PDF Text in Word |
|---|
| சுப்ரமணியன் |
| ெ◌தாை◌லக்காட்சித் |
| குப்ை◌ேபமடுகள் |
| சிேவநசபுரத்ை◌தப் |
| நடுே◌வ |
| ே◌காயில் |
| படி |
| ை◌வத்தது |

Fig. 20.4A: TU PDF Extracted in Word

| |
|---|
| சுப்ரமணியன் |
| தொலைக்காட்சித் |
| குப்பைமேடுகள் |
| சிவநேசபுரத்தைப் |
| நடுவே |
| கோயில் |
| படி |
| வைத்தது |

Fig. 20.4B: TACE16 PDF Extracted in Word.

Hence Tamil Unicode text stored in PDF standard is unreliable. The data integrity is totally lost in a round trip PDF storage and retrieval cycle even from MS Word. This is a major drawback for not only print and publishing but also for all office and commercial applications where PDF is used as data storage and exchange format.

***Solutions***: Unlike Tamil Unicode, TACE16 stores all data as Simple Script without the use of the modifiers. All characters are stored as a single unit and there is no need for the OS to do the Glyph reordering process. Tamil text in TACE16 when stored in PDF, the internal storage order of PDF matches with the TACE16 ordering. On extraction of TACE16 from stored PDF documents, the data integrity is strictly maintained. TACE16 is found to be very reliable for round trip PDF storage and retrieval cycle. Production trials in real time publishing environment also proved its reliability with all applications like MS Word, Adobe, Quark and Corel in both Windows and MacOSX. (Fig. 20.4B)

### *Tamil Spell Checking*

Automatic spell checking is a tool used extensively by not only the print and publishing but also by all office and commercial applications. Spell Checkers indicate not only spelling errors but also sandhi errors which is common in Tamil. Some of the text control tools used by the developers of Tamil Spell checkers do not support TU. Dual representation of certain characters in TU creates problems to the spell checking tools in identifying the words and its component parts. Most of the Spell checking engines use their own internal storage format for processing the text. This creates an additional burden in converting the Unicode text to internal encoding and after processing reconverting to Unicode format. This may affect the efficiency of the spell checking process to a great extent.

***Solutions***: TACE16 with all Tamil characters encoded with one to one mapping and without any complex rendering process is supported in all text control engines. In TACE16, there is no dual representation of any Tamil character. Hence TACE16 can be used as the internal encoding for processing also. The vowels and consonants are easily identified from their code values, which enhances the text processing speed considerably. Tamil Spell checking tools based on TACE16 not only work well with all current applications but also found to be far more efficient as compared to tools based on Tamil

Unicode. Processing speed is very critical in production environments like newspapers.

### Tamil Hyphenation and Justification

Hyphenation and justification for Tamil text is far more complex than English. For English as the Hyphenation dictionaries are generally built into most of the professional applications, the hyphenation process is simple and automatic. For Tamil, there are no standard hyphenation dictionaries available. In a multi-column newspaper or magazine publication, hyphenation and justification is very critical. Improper word breaking at the end of each line will give very awkward look. Normally it is essential to do the manual hyphenation break at appropriate places. In real life production environment, reformatting and repagination are quite common. At each reformatting stage, the hyphenation breaking needs to be redone. All the earlier hyphenation breaks need to be removed as word breaks in middle of the lines is not allowed. With TU some of the complex characters can break in between the characters resulting in illegal breaks.

*Solutions*: Auto hyphenation for Tamil is normally achieved by plug-ins to applications like In design, etc; A series of hyphenation rules are built into the plug-ins, which automates this tedious manual process. While applying these hyphenation rules, it is important to ensure that illegal breaks do not happen in between complex characters. With Tamil Unicode, the bit length varies from character to character and hence this process is little more complex. Whereas with TACE16, all characters are having uniform bit length, the process is much simpler. Also the possibility of illegal character break is totally eliminated inTACE16, as all characters are represented by a single code point.

### Challenges in e-Governance with Tamil Unicode

Most of the e-Governance projects require people involvement and interaction at grass-root level. Local language enabling in an efficient method is essential for the successful implementation of e-Governance projects. An end to end e-Governance project will involve multiple media which include web, print, mobile, palm readers, kiosks and e-Books. The data should travel reliably across multiple operating systems and databases. The documents should be viewable, portable, text extractable for local processing and printable as and when required. The system should provide for reliable and efficient long term storage of data, which are independent of operating systems or applications. The system should provide a reliable and easy to use search and retrieval of the documents.

Tamil Unicode implementation in E-Governance is faced with a series of challenges. TU support is lacking in several media like print, mobile, ebooks, palm readers and broadcast. Wherever the documents need to be published in printed form, the documents need to be converted back to legacy 8-bit encoding. This increases the risk of errors and necessitates manual proofreading and correction.

Integrating mobile, which is the most widely used device in the grassroot level, poses several limitations with TU due to lack of support for complex rendering in all devices uniformly. Also reliable data portability across operating systems and applications is doubtful, as the TU support is incomplete in several applications. Dual representation of certain complex characters poses problems to database sorting and indexing, resulting in inefficient search and retrieval of documents. Long term storage of portable documents with TU in PDF format is unreliable, as data integrity on retrieval can't be ensured. Also the stored data in text and other formats can't be retrieved without the help of the respective rendering engine (like Uniscribe in MS) provided by the respective operating system. This is a threat to data security in case of discontinuity of support for particular rendering engine by the OS provider after some years.

***Solutions***: TACE16 was tested by the National Informatics Center (NIC), GoI, as part of the testing process of TN Task

Force on All Character Encoding in many of the E-Governance applications and confirmed its usability. Hence TACE16 could be used safely in all E-Governance applications where Unicode support is lacking or doubtful.

### Font design for Multilingual Publishing

Unicode provides code points for all languages of the world including Indian languages. This give the provision for keeping multiple language scripts in a single font. (e.g. Arial Unicode). One can design a font with both TU and TACE16 in the same font, which will give many operational advantages where both are required. This will help the user to read the TU text and convert to TACE16 when necessary for printing without the need for changing the font. Publishers of multilingual dictionary, commercial applications which require multilingual user interface and government departments which need to create documents in multiple languages can create a font with the required language scripts to suit their special needs. This is one of the major advantages of Unicode as compared to legacy 8-bit encoding.

### e-Paper Publishing

In todays condition Newspapers and magazine publishers who are using professional publishing applications will be forced to use TACE16 until TU support is available. Publishers who are publishing e-Paper version of their publication in the web (Electronic Paper in Newspaper look and feel) can use TACE16 encoding itself without the need to convert to TU. This gives the advantage of better access speed to the web readers. They also provide archived older newspapers for their readers. The extend of old archived E-papers one can provide depends on the online storage space provided in the Web Server. With TACE16, one can provide much longer period of newspaper archives online with available space.

### *Mobile Publishing*

Today's newspapers do not stop with print medium, but extend to mobile for quicker delivery of hotnews and headlines. Tamil Unicode support in mobile devices across brands and models is still a distant reality. This is due to the difficulty in accommodating the overload of complex rendering necessary for TU. TACE16 being a simple script without any complex rendering, can be used easily and efficiently in mobile publishing.

### *e-Book Publishing*

Book publishers may be using TACE16 due to lack of TU support in publishing applications. Just like in mobile devices, e-Book readers also lack the capability to handle the complex rendering required for TU. Here again TACE16 has proved its usefulness in field testing with few manufacturers.

### *Broadcast Media*

Many media houses today are planning to integrate their newsroom for print with broadcast studios in order to provide cross media news coverage. They use special purpose titling and editing tools, which are yet to provide TU support. In these situations, TACE16 will be useful, as all these broadcast applications support simple scripts like TACE16.

## Conclusion

Publishing and e-Governance, though faced with several challenges in implementing Tamil Unicode, they can be overcome to a great extent by use of the TACE16 encoding wherever TU support is lacking and by using suitable pulg-ins for encoding conversion, spell checking and hyphenation tools.

21

# Prediction of Pauses in TTS-Tamil

— *P. Arulmozhi and A.G. Ramakrishnan*


***ABSTRACT***

*Text to Speech (TTS) involves the task of converting text typed in electronic format into a speech signal. In MILE lab, we are involved in making a TTS system for Tamil and Kannada. In this chapter, the contribution of syntactic information such as Part of Speech (PoS) Tags in enhancing the quality of a Text to Speech (TTS) synthesis system for Tamil is researched. The quality of a TTS system is measured by the intelligibility and naturalness of the synthesized speech. The NLP module of the TTS system (for example, text normalization) contributes to not only to its intelligibility, but also to its naturalness, by improving the prosody. The stress and pause modelling can be improved using the PoS and other syntactic information. In a sentence, where there should be a pause, and where there should not be a pause has to be identified for the naturalness of the produced speech. Because, a sentence without pause or with identical pause intervals sounds robotic. Also, pause at a wrong place makes the sentence unnatural and there is a possibility of change of meaning. For example take the following sentence,*

*avarukku inRu <P> mAlai kitaittatu.*

*avarukku inRu mAlai <P> kitaittatu.*

*<P> here indicates that there should be a pause. The pause given in different places give different meanings. Syntactic information such as Parts of Speech (PoS) can be used for identifying the rules for pause in a particular sentence. A rule based PoS tagger is developed for this purpose without using a root word dictionary. Currently, manual evaluation shows an accuracy of approximately 74 per cent using only the lexical rules. The performance is expected to improve after the context sensitive rules are applied. Rules are made for predicting the insertion of pause at the right place. The manual evaluation of pause insertion shows a significant improvement in the naturalness of the produced sentence.*

## Introduction

This chapter presents a rule based Parts of Speech (PoS) tagging method in the perspective of improving the naturalness in the synthesized speech. The quality of a TTS system is measured by the intelligibility and naturalness of the synthesized speech. There are two main modules in a TTS system. One is the Natural Language Processing (NLP) module, which takes care of the production of phonetic transcription, intonation and rhythm. Another is the Digital Signal Processing (DSP) module which takes care of the production of the speech wave-form of the given text. The stress and pause in the speech contribute majorly to the naturalness, which is controlled by the NLP module. Using this PoS tagger, we try to find out the right place to introduce pause in the synthesized speech. Introducing a high degree of naturalness is theoretically possible, but the rules to do so are still to be discovered (Jonathan A. 1996 Many linguistic aspects are analyzed (Thierry D) and syntactic information such as POS tagging is considered important to achieve a good TTS. In this paper, we present a POS tagger created for Tamil, which is a highly agglutinative and partially free word order language.

## PoS Taggers

The purpose of a PoS tagger is to automatically find out the syntactic category of a word in a sentence. Different methods may be followed to do PoS tagging. Most commonly used are rule based, statistical, and transformation based methods. Rule based taggers work on predefined linguistic rules for deciding the syntactic category of a word in a sentence. These rules may be lexical or context sensitive and they are language dependent. Statistical taggers work on the calculated probability, in which a PoS tag for a particular word is decided based on the lexical and contextual probability. A training corpus is used to train the system and the input sentence is tagged based on the probability which is calculated using the training corpus. Transformation based taggers derive rules based on learning. Those rules are used to find the syntactic category. In English, Brill's tagger is the most commonly used, TBL based tagger. There are statistical, rule based and hybrid taggers being worked on for Tamil (Arulmozhi P, Sobha L, 2006).

## MILE PoS Tagger for Tamil

### *Purpose of MILE Tagger*

In natural speech, we introduce stress and pause at the right places, so that it is easily understandable. In a TTS system, the DSP component produces the speech wave-form and the NLP component is responsible for the naturalness of the produced speech. It should identify the right places to introduce pause. The amount of pause to be introduced has been identified. The pause is introduced using the category of the words in a sentence. Other syntactic information such as shallow parsing and clause boundary identification will be helpful not only in identifying pause, but also to find out the pitch and intonation.

There are a few PoS taggers available for Tamil. They have been developed for the purpose of preprocessing for NLP activities such as machine translation and information extraction (Arulmozhi P. *et.al* 2004). The probability based PoS taggers need huge training corpus. They provide the PoS tags according to the tagset used for training. In the case of a TTS, we do not need such detailed tagging.

### *Nature of Tamil Language*

Tamil is a morphologically rich, agglutinative and partially free word order language. Compound words are common in this language, where two or more words are combined to form a single word. The case markers and tense markers appear as inflections of the root word itself. For example, taking the word 'varukirAn', the inflections and root word can be split as follows.

vA + kir + An

vA - root word

kir - present tense marker

An - 3rd person, Singular, Neuter gender.

Tamil is a partially free word order language because changing the word order to some extent does not affect the meaning of the sentence. However, this order change cannot occur within a phrase. For the sentence,

1 'Aciriyar nanRAka paTitta mANavanukku paricae kotuttAr'

Teacher thoroughly studied Student+Dat prize+Acc gave+Hon

The teacher gave the prize to the student who studied thoroughly.

It can be written as

1'nanRAka paTitta mANavanukku Aciriyar paricae kotuttAr'

2 'Aciriyar paricae nanRAka paTitta mANavanukku kotuttAr'

but,

1 *'Aciriyar paTitta mANavanukku paricae nanRAka kotuttAr'

changes the meaning. So, within a phrase, the word order does not change.

### *Tagset*

A tagset is the set of all tags used by the PoS tagger. There are two levels of tags—the main tags and sub tags. The main tags identify the main category of the word such as noun verb or adjective. The subtags identify the category of the inflections such as person, number, gender, and tense. For the purpose of TTS, we do not need very detailed tags unlike other NLP activities. But using only the main tags would not give sufficient information. So we need some of the sub tags too. So, as a special case, we have developed a tagset for the purpose of inserting pause in a sentence. In our tagset, each tag is a combination of a main tag and one or more sub-tags. The nouns take the case and plural markers and the verbs take person, number, gender, and tense markings. Apart from this, pronouns have person, number, and gender. The clitics are suffixed to the root word to form adverbs and conjunctions. Then the dates, numbers, and punctuations are also tagged separately. English PoS taggers and some of the Tamil taggers (Dhanalakshmi V. *et. al.* 2009) use monadic tags. Monadic tags do not give information on inflections, which is important for TTS. We use structured tags such as "NN+pl.acc" in which different pieces of information serve in different parts of the rules. This tag means, a noun in with the inflection for plural and accusative. We have 15 main tags and 30 subtags adding up to 45 tags.

## *MILE Tagger*

PoS Tagger. This PoS tagger is a rule based one. We do not use a root word dictionary. The tagger is based on a two stage architecture. The block diagram of the PoS tagger is shown in Figure 21.1.

In the block diagram, each block explains its functionality. The first stage has the lexical rules and the second stage has the context sensitive rules. First, a sentence is taken as input and split into tokens. For each token, the suffixes are identified. Then, using the lexical rules, which work at the word level, each word is assigned a PoS tag according to the suffixes identified.

Then, this output is given as an input to the second stage, where the context sensitive rules change the tag if it is wrongly tagged by the lexical rules. Thus, the final tagged sentence is obtained. Separate tables are created for programming purpose with the list of suffixes identified. A lexical rule looks like,

2*1+1*1, NN+pl.acc

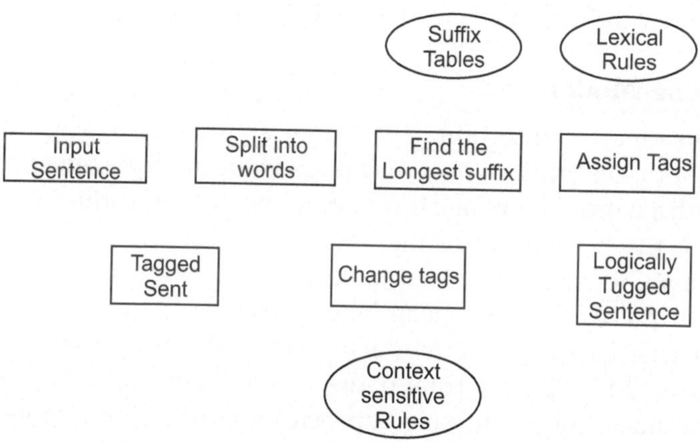


**Fig. 21.1.**

This means, the suffixes indexed 2*1 (Suffix Table 2 Column 1 - kaL) and 1*1 (Suffix Table 1 Column 1 - ae) occur in a sequence, the word will be tagged as Noun+Plural+ Accusative. Here 'kaL' is the plural marker and 'ae' is the accusative marker. There are 13 such tables which list 103 suffixes identified and put in. These suffixes are used by the lexical rules. The context sensitive rules are embedded in the system. For example the following can be considered as a context sensitive rule.

'If a sentence starts with a verb, change it to noun'.

Since Tamil is a verb ending language, a sentence can-not start with a verb. So, if the first word of a sentence is wrongly tagged as a verb in the first level, it will be corrected in the second level. The combinations of lexical rules including the inflections are 533 and the number of context sensitive rules are 4.

For any PoS tagger to work correctly, the sentence boundaries have to be identified. We use a sentence splitter for splitting paragraphs to sentences. Input to the sentence splitter is any Tamil text such as paragraphs. The output is an array of sentences. This process is also embedded in the PoS tagger based on our need. We use a rule based sentence splitter and the rules are heuristic in nature.

## Pause Model

Pause model. Insertion of the right amount of pauses at the right places adds to the naturalness of the synthesized speech. With a natural language text, native speakers introduce pauses with the knowledge of the language acquired. But in a TTS system, those pauses need to be inserted by the system at the right places. For European languages such as Spanish, there are rule based pause models developed and experimented (Rafael M 2002). A wrong pause inserted between two words may make the synthesized speech unnatural. For simplicity, such an example sentence is illustrated in English. Here, the notation <np> denotes "no pause" between the words, whereas <p> refers to the required pause.

***Example***

The< np> book<np>is<p> on<np>the<np>table.

The<np>book<np>is<np> on<p>the<np>table.

Speech synthesized as per the tags for the first sentence will appear perceptually natural, whereas for the second sentence, a wrong pause between words 'on' and 'the' will appear perceptually unnatural. Hence PoS information and pause are very important in the context of TTS. In this chapter, we focus on pause insertion between successive words by pause prediction from the PoS tags estimated from the input text. Presently we use key words and heuristic rules for inserting pauses. Rules for inserting pauses at the right places are created according to the PoS tags.

At present, in the syntactic level, only PoS tags are considered for identifying pauses. It is considered as a basic preprocessing needed. On top of this, the phrase chunks may be identified, and that will be useful in identifying the places where pause must be inserted. In that process, the phonological phrases must be identified finally for identifying pauses and intonation.

Six levels of pause have been identified, which determine the duration of the pause. In Chinese pause model, they use minor, major, and punctuation breaks (Fu-chiang *et.al* 1997). We have defined <P0>, <P1>, <P2>, <P3>, <P4>, and <PW>. P0: No pause, P1: Lowest pause, P2: Medium Pause (Ex: Pause after a comma), P3: Significant Pause (Ex: Pause after a semicolon), P4: Highest Pause (Ex. Pause between sentences). The pause levels P0 to P4 are derived form the existing synthesis database. This work has been carried out for Tamil and can be extended to all Dravidian languages with no major change. <PW> is the common pause between each word. Wherever <P0>... <P4> is not identified, <PW> is assumed.

At the initial level, <PW> is assumed for each word, and rules for converting it to <P0> to <P4> is made.

The sample rules are given below.

1. There is no pause (or may be very minimal pause) between a number and certain words following, such as 'mani', 'latcam', 'kOTi'. There is a list of words defined for this rule. Any noun in plural form, (NN+PL) after a number does not have a pause.
2. If the previous word has an accusative/dative marker, and the current word is a postposition, there is no pause between the current and the previous words. Ex : avanai <P0> pola, avanukku <P0> pin
3. Combine the words with POS tags Adjectival Participle (AJP) and Noun (NN - any number of them) occurring together. There is no pause between them.
4. There should be a pause before quantifier (Q). Ex : (azhakiya kiraamamum)<P3>(oru periya ooraa Tciyum)

There are 15 such rules made for converting <PW> to <P0> - <P4>. In natural speech, we do not give any pause between most of the words. Taking that into consideration, we did another experiment. Instead of taking <PW>as default pause, we took <P0> as default ie. There is no pause between any word initially, and then inserting pauses using rules. This reduced the rule set from 15 to 8, because we had more rules for <P0>. The output from both is obtained and given for evaluation.

## Output and Evaluation

The output of the system contains the original sentence, the predicted PoS tags and the predicted pause levels. All are displayed parallely. An example output is shown in Figure 21.2.

In the figure, the first line is the Tamil input; second line is the corresponding meaning in English; third line is the predicted PoS tags and the fourth line is the pause levels identified.

| சி.பி.எஸ்.இ. | முறையில் | படிக்கும் | மாணவர்களுக்கு | அடுத்த |
|---|---|---|---|---|
| C.B.S.E | stream+loc | studying | students+pl+dat | next |
| NN | NN+loc | VB+fut+3sn | NN+pl+dat | AJP |
| <P0> | <PW> | <PW> | <PW> | <P0> |

| கல்வி | ஆண்டு | முதல் | 10ம் | வகுப்பு | தேர்வு | கிடையாது |
|---|---|---|---|---|---|---|
| education | year | from | 10th | class | exam | No |
| NN | NN | PP | Q | NN | NN | VB+pst+3sn+neg |
| <P0> | <P0> | <P2> | <P0> | <P0> | <PW> | <P4> |

**Fig. 21.2.**

This output is given to the DSP module and the wave form of the sentence obtained. The people who evaluated the outputs are native Tamil speakers, who did not have knowledge about the methods used for creating TTS outputs. 3 types of outputs are given to the evaluators and Mean Opinion Score (MOS) is obtained. 10 sentences are spoken by the TTS as follows:

Without implementing the pause model

After implementing the pause model with default as <PW>

After implementing the pause model with default as <P0>

The scores are given from 1-5 according to the understandability and naturalness (1-worst, 5-best). The evaluation based on the mean opinion score gives encouraging results. The rule based PoS tagger is evaluated manually for the correctness of the tags. The evaluation is done manually. In a given tag, if the main tag is correct and the sub-tag is wrong, or vice versa, we take that as a wrong tag. The system gives 78 per cent results without a root word dictionary. More context sensitive rules are to be added so that the accuracy of the POS tagger also can be improved.

## REFERENCES

1. Arulmozhi. P, Sobha. L, Kumara Shanmugam. B. 2004. Parts of Speech Tagger for Tamil. In the *Proceedings of Symposium on Indian Morphology, Phonology and Language Engineering*, (March 19-21) Indian Institute of Technology, Kharagpur (pp. 55-57).

2. Arulmozhi Palanisamy and Sobha Lalitha Devi. 2006. HMM-based POS Tagger for a Relatively Free Word Order Language. *A Poster Presentation in CICLing-06* (February 19-25) at Mexico.

3. Brill, E. 1995 Transformation-based Error-driven Learning and Natural Language Processing: *A Case Study in Parts-of-Speech Tagging*. Computational Linguistics, 21, 4 (pp. 543-565).

4. Dhanalakshmi V, Anand Kumar M and Soman K P, 2009. PoS Tagger and Chunker for Tamil Language. *Tamil Internet Conference*, Cologne, Germany. pp. 250-255.

5. Fu-chiang Chou', Chiu-yu Tseng, Keh-jiann Chen, and Lin-shan Lee 1997. *A Chinese Text-to-Speech System Based on Parts-of-Speech Analysis*, Prosodic Modelling and non-Uniform Units. ICASSP'97, Volume – 2, Munich, Germany.

6. Jonathan Allen 1993. Linguistic Aspects of Speech Synthesis. Presented at a Coloquium entitled 'Human-Machine Communication by Voice. Organized by Lawrence R. Rabiner, held by the National Academy of Sciences at The Arnold and Mabel Beckman Center in Irvine, CA.

7. Rafael Marin, Lourdes Aguilar, David Casacuberta, 2002. Placing Pauses in Read Spoken Spanish: A Model and An Algorithm. Language Design: *Journal of Theoretical and Experimental Linguistics*, pp. 49-67.

8. Thierry Dutoit. *High-quality Text-to-speech Synthesis: An Overview.* Faculte Polytechnique de Mons, TCTS Lab, 31, bvd Dolez, B-7000 MONS, Belgium.

# 22

# Text Analysing and Retrieval System Using Tamil Phonemes and Vector Space Model

— *Premalatha, R. and Srinivasan, S.*

**ABSTRACT**

*Intelligent information retrieval is one of the important topics in the 21st century. In Tamil documents, generally, morphology (separating noun and verb) concept is used to retrieve the text. In this system we use Tamil phonology so that we can widen our search criteria namely, Vowel—Short, Long; Consonant—Vallinam(Hard), Mellinam (Soft) and Idaiyanam (Medium). So the system would search quickly. Hence the performance of the system would increase. In the classical system, the user should give the exact word to retrieve the information. But in TAR system, as the system internally has its spell checker, the misspelled word can be corrected and also the information can be retrieved. This would be useful for Tamil literates, Tamil students, Tamil learners, etc..*

## Introduction

For thousands of years people have realized the importance of archiving and finding information. With the advent of computers, it became possible to store large amount of information and finding useful information from such collections which became a necessity. The field of IR was born in the 1950s out of this necessity. Over the last forty years, the field has matured considerably. Several IR systems[9] are used on an everyday basis by a wide variety of users. The need for information retrieval[1] arises in the

Tamil literature documents from the ancient era to the latest, which helps in sharing the data through the internet. In this chapter, we are going to do text analyzing and retrieval system using Tamil phonemes and vector space model[8]. In this system, searches can be done in three ways namely: (*i*) Main topics searches; (*ii*) Subtitle searches; and (*iii*) Keyword searches.

The input word would be given in Tamil using Tamil virtual keyboard. In the classical system, the system[4] read the whole word and it identified whether the word is a noun or a verb. Finally it found the word from the database. In the past it took a lot of time for retrieval. Because in the older system once the entire word is entered, the system would do the searching process. But in the proposed system, the system would not wait for the entire word to enter; perhaps the searching process starts immediately after the first letter is entered. Because the system performs the search processes for every letter of a word. This approach considerably increases the speed of the retrieval process.

***Tamil language*:** Tamil is the oldest and truest of the Dravidian speeches. Tamil boasts its literary tradition for more than 2,200 years. Tamil is the most remarkable body of secular poetry extant in India (Tamil is a South Indian language spoken widely in Tamil Nadu in India). Tamil has the longest unbroken literary tradition amongst the Dravidian

Languages. Tamil[1] has 12 vowels and 18 consonants. They combined with each other to yield 216 composite characters and 1 special character (aayutha ezhuthu). Summing up there are 247 letters in standard Tamil alphabet.

***Tamil literature***: It has a rich and long literary tradition spanning more than two thousand years. Contributors to the Tamil literature are mainly from Tamil people from Tamil Nadu, Sri Lankan Tamils from Sri Lanka and from Tamil Diasporas. A revival of Tamil literature took place from the late nineteenth century when works of religious and philosophical nature were written in a style that made it easier for the common people to enjoy. Nationalist poets began to utilize the power of poetry in influencing the masses. With the growth of literacy, Tamil prose began to blossom and mature.

## Literature Survey

Language occupies an important position in the history of Indian cultural traditions. The central Government declared Tamil as one of the classical languages on September 17, 2004. Information retrieval[2] of Tamil literature is a difficult work to do because it was used in olden period Tamil format and it was on poetry format as well. Generally morphology approaches[3] are used for information retrieval of Tamil documents (Anand Kumar M), 2009. An IR system returns a list of long documents to a user query. The construction and use of exploration models and search indices consumes processing time, memory, and disk space. Furthermore, in real systems any search and exploration methods must be computationally efficient. In particular, the delay perceived by the users is critical.

It is therefore important to develop methods that can speed up the search process while maintaining high perceived quality, particularly in the range of high precision and low recall which is most crucial in actual user settings. The TAR system is suitable for performing information retrieval using

Tamil phonemes and vector space model that were organized for exploration of Tamil document collections.

## Tamil Phonemes

Native grammarians classify Tamil phonemes into vowels, consonants, and a 'secondary character', the aytam.

***Vowels***: There are 12 vowels in Tamil, called uyireluttu (uyir - life, eluttu - letter). These vowels are classified into short (kuril) and long (Nedil), five of each type and two diphthongs, /ai/ and /au/, and three 'shortened' (kurriyl) vowels. The long vowels are about twice as long as the short vowels. The diphthongs are usually pronounced about 1.5 times as long as the short vowels.

***Consonants***: Consonants are known as meyyeluttu (mey – body, eluttu – letters) in Tamil. It is classified into three categories with six in each category: vallinam (hard), mellinam (soft or Nasal) and itayinam (medium).

## System Architecture

In the TAR system, 4 phases are used. They are: (*i*) Classification; (*ii*) Analyzer; (*iii*) Retrieval; and (iv) Spell Checker.

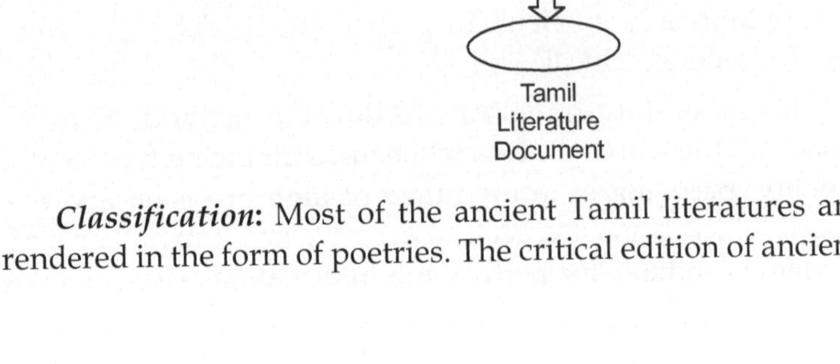


***Classification***: Most of the ancient Tamil literatures are rendered in the form of poetries. The critical edition of ancient

Tamil works include 41 works namely: (1) Thirukkural; (2) Pura naanooru; (3) Aga naanooru; (4) Silapathigaram; (5) Seevaga chinathamani; (6) Manimegalai; (7) Kundalakesi; (8) Valayapathi; (9) Padhinen Mel kanakku (18 Upper Classics); (10) Padhinen Keezh kanakku (18 Lower Classics) etc. Since most of the Ancient Tamil works are in poetry and in anthology forms, a Main class is derived with 41 categories[10] and each category has various sub divisions. The sub divisions are classified as Main topics, Subtitles and Keywords.

***Analyzer***: Every letter has been analyzed by the analyzer using Tamil phonology[2]. If a key is pressed through the Tamil virtual keyboard, the analyzer would identify the letter through any one of the following: Vowels(V) or Consonants (C). Vowels are again classified into two types, Kuril(k) and Nedil(n). Similarly consonants are classified into three classes with 6 in each class and are called Vallinam(v), Idaiyinam(i) and Mellinam(m). Once the letter is identified, it locates the letter from the Database. The cycle would continue until all the letters in the word are processed. The index position should change for every letter until the complete word is entered.

**Eg:** புகழ் -: பு → ப் + உ, க → க் + அ, ழ் → ழ்

(C-v) + (V-k) (C-v) + (V-k) (C-m)

***Retrieval***: In the retrieval module[12], once the word is found in indices, it retrieves the poem and its explanations from the documents using vector space model[3]. The performance of the search are increased by splitting up the category by 3 ways namely: (*i*) Main topics searches; (*ii*) Subtitles searches Analyzer Retrieval Classification and Indexing Poem and its explanation Input Keyword (Identifying Tamil Phonemes) Tamil Literature Document; and (*iii*) Keyword searches. For example, if the input is given from 'Main topics', then the subtitle and keyword could be skipped.

***Spell Checker***: The spell checker basically checks the spelling of the given word. If the word is wrong or the word is not in the DB, then it would suggest some other word related to the input. Generally the user cannot enter the first letter wrongly, but he may do mid of the word for the letters like

1) ர ற 2) ல ள ழ 3) ண ன ந

So the spell checker is designed in such a way that the first letter would be skipped and the rest of the letters in the word should undergo the spell-check. Basically it skips the first letter of the word and check the rest of the letters of the word. Finally it gets the word from the DB and replaces it. If there is more than one combination, it would list all possible combinations to select. Look at these examples below:

**Case: 1** பயண் → பயன்; அரிதல் → அறிதல்

**Case: 2** புகல் , புகள் → புகழ் **Case: 3** தளை → தலை, தழை

## Vector Space Model

In the vector space model[11], we represent documents as vectors. Term weighting is an important aspect of modern text retrieval systems. Terms are words, phrases, or any other indexing units used to identify the contents of a text. Since different terms have different importance in a text, an important indicator—the term weight[8]—is associated with every term. The retrieval performance of the information retrieval system is largely dependent on similarity measures. Furthermore, a term weighting scheme plays an important role for the similarity measure. There are three components in a weighting scheme is

$$a_{ij} = g_i * t_{ij} * d_j$$

Where $g_i$ is the global weight of the ith term, $t_{ij}$ is the local weight of the ith term in the jth document, $d_j$ is the normalization factor for the jth document. Usually the two main components that affect the importance of a term in a text are the term frequency factor[13] (tf ), the inverse document frequency factor.

**TFIDF weighting:** TFIDF is the most common weighting method used to describe documents in the Vector Space Model[12], particularly in IR problems. we assign to each term in a document a weight for that term, that depends on the number of occurrences of the term in the document. In addition, IDF measures how infrequent a word is in the collection. This value is estimated using the whole training text collection at hand. The simplest approach is to assign the weight to be equal to the number of occurrences of term t in document d.

$$\text{weight } t,d = \log(\text{tf } t,d + 1) \log_{xt} n$$

where tft, *d* is the frequency of word *t* in document *d*, *n* is the number of documents in the text collection and *xt* is the number of documents where word *t* occurs. Normalization to unit length is generally applied to the resulting vectors.

## Evaluation

Objective evaluation of search effectiveness has been a cornerstone of IR. Progress in the field critically depends upon experimenting with new ideas and evaluating the effects of these ideas, especially given the experimental nature of the field. Since the early years, it was evident to researchers in the community that objective evaluation of search techniques would play a key role in the field. The two desired properties that have been accepted by the research community for measurements of search effectiveness are recall:[3] the proportion of relevant documents retrieved by the system; and precision: the proportion of retrieved documents those are relevant.

Experiments Results: Information retrieval systems comparison:

**Input words is புகழ்**

| Title | Recall | Precision |
|---|---|---|
| IT using Merphology | 0.41 | 0.44 |
| IR using phonology | 0.50 | 0.51 |

**Recall / Precision**

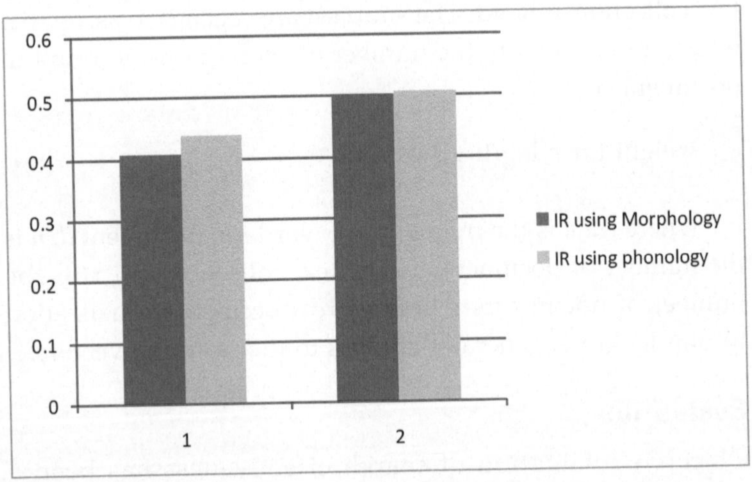


## Conclusion

The TAR system would be pretty much helpful for all Tamil literates and students to search and learn. The TAR system focuses on Tamil phonemes. Also performance tuning has also been done in the system. In addition with that, the TAR system has the spell checker concept which makes the system to search the data reasonably quick. This system currently supports 41 categories alone. In addition to this we can further add more documents in future. However this concept will be designed more useful to the users, in future.

## REFERENCES


1. Abirami.S and D. Manjula, Enabling Intelligent Information Retrieval from Tamil Document Images, *Asian Journal of Information Technology*, 996-1000, 2006
2. Abirami.S and D. Manjula, Feature String-based Intelligent Information Retrieval from Tamil Document Images, International Journal of Computer Applications in Technology,Publication, Volume 35,150-164, 2009
3. Amit Singhal,Google, Modern Information Retrieval: A Brief Overview, IEEE tranactions, IEEE Computer Society Technical Committee on Data Engineering, 2001
4. Anand Kumar M, Dhanalakshmi V, Rajendran S, Soman K P, A Novel Approach to Morphological Analysis for Tamil Language, Internet Tamil Conference, 2009
5. Bayardo, R. J., Ma, Y., & Srikant, R. Scaling-up All Pairs Similarity Search. In Proceedings of the 16th *International Conference on World Wide Web* (WWW '07), pp. 131-140, New York, 2007
6. Gorman.J, & Curran J. R., Scaling Distributional Similarity to Large Corpora. In *Proceedings of the 21st International Conference on Computational Linguistics and the 44th annual meeting of the Association for Computational Linguistics*, pp. 361-368, 2006.
7. Guo xian tan, Chsitian vivard, Alex.c, Information Retrieval Model for Online Handwritten Script Identification, International Conference on Document Analysis and Recognition,Spain, 2009
8. Holger, Billhardt, Victor Maojo, A Context Vector Model for Information Retrieval, *Journal of the American Society for Information Science and Technology*, Volume 53, Pages: 236 - 249, Year of Publication: 2002
9. Massimo Melucci, A Basis for Information Retrieval in Context, *ACM Transactions on Information Systems* (ToIS), volume.26 n.3, p.1-41, June 2000
10. Rajan.K,Ramalingam.V, M.Ganesh, Automatic Classification of Tamil Documents Using Vector Space Model and Artificial Neural Network, *Expert Systems with Applications: An International Journal*, Volume 36, Issue 8 Pages: 10914-10918, 2009
11. Ray Larson, Marc Davis. *SIMS 202: Information Organization and Retrieval.* UC Berkeley SIMS, Lecture 18: Vector Representation, 2002.
12. Wan, V. N. Anh, I. Takigawa, and H. Mamitsuka. *Combining Vector-space and Word-based Aspect Models for Passage Retrieval.* In E. M. Voorhees and L. P. Buckland, editors, Proc. 15th Text Retrieval Conference (TREC 2006), Special Publication 500-272, November 2006.

23

# Speaking Tool in Tamil for Vocally Disabled

*— Shashikiran, K. and Swapnil Belhe*

## Introduction

It has always been a challenge to bridge the gap between vocally disabled and the masses. The development of sign language has only been partially successful in bridging the gap. It requires persons conversing to know the sign language. Our work is a conscious effort to overcoming this pitfall. The proposed methodology is a combination of two different entities namely (Online Handwriting Recognition) OHR and (Text to Speech) TTS. OHR deals with recognition of handwritten words online. In an on-line handwriting recognition system, machine recognizes the writing while the user writes. The OHR output is in Tamil Unicode and becomes the input to TTS. Unicode is a globally accepted encoding format which makes our application viable to be used in various circumstances. TTS is a system that takes Unicode text and produces natural and intelligible speech in that language. This enables the patients, who had laryngectomy and tracheotomy as well as the vocally challenged to communicate effectively. As vocal disability may be congenital or because of ailments like oral or throat cancer, our method serves equally to both.

The tool is based on a hand-held, Tablet PC based on Intel Atom processor. The user can write one sentence at a time on the screen using the stylus and then click the button 'Speak'. The sentence is recognized and then converted into speech and spoken out. Thus, the patient can call the attention of the nurses or his relatives in another room easily.

## Details of the OHR Module

In Online handwriting recognition, a machine recognizes, as a user writes on a pressure sensitive screen with a stylus. The stylus captures information about the position of the pen tip as a sequence of points in time. The sequence of point between a PEN DOWN and PEN UP signal defines a stroke. This spatiotemporal information of the character being traced is the only input available to the online recognition system. Also given a character, one can capture the different writing styles using the information from the stylus.

Given a Tamil word, we first run a segmentation algorithm to identify the individual symbols. This algorithm segments word level data into symbol level data, as the modeling of the data is done at the symbol level. The recognition is performed at this level and results are concatenated to form the words.

The extracted symbols are subject to the following preprocessing modules: smoothing to remove noise, resampling to a fixed number of points for speed normalization and size normalization.

Once symbols are brought to a standardized form, a set of seven features namely ,

| | |
|---|---|
| Pre-processed N&Y co-ordinates | Preprocessed data points (xy) are themselves good features |
| Pen direction angle | At each sample point, the direction of pen tip movement from that point tot he next point can be used as a feature |
| Normalized first derivatives of X & Y | Derived at each sample point of the preprocessed Tamil symbol, are also used |
| Normalized Second derivatives of X & Y | Same as above |

The preprocessing techniques and features are discussed elaborately in Rituraj *et al*[2]. These features are then fed to the SDTW classifier for recognition of the Tamil symbol.

Statistical Dynamic Time warping (SDTW): In SDTW, a reference character is represented by a sequence Q=(Q1;Q2;Q3;Qlq) of statistical quantities (states), as shown in Fig 23.1.

These statistical quantities include

1. Discrete probabilities that statistically mode the transitions between states. We have empirically used 20 states in our work.
2. A continuous probability density function that models the feature distribution at each state. We have modelled this distribution as a multivariate Gaussian distribution for each of the 20 states.

While testing, the SDTW distance of test pattern to the reference model of each class is computed. and the test pattern is assigned the label of the class giving minimum SDTW distance. The definition of SDTW distance is different from that of DTW and is given in Claus *et al*[1]. Fig.1 shows how the matching takes place between the reference model and Test pattern. Matrix in Fig. 23.1 shows the DTW path (path of best SDTW matching).

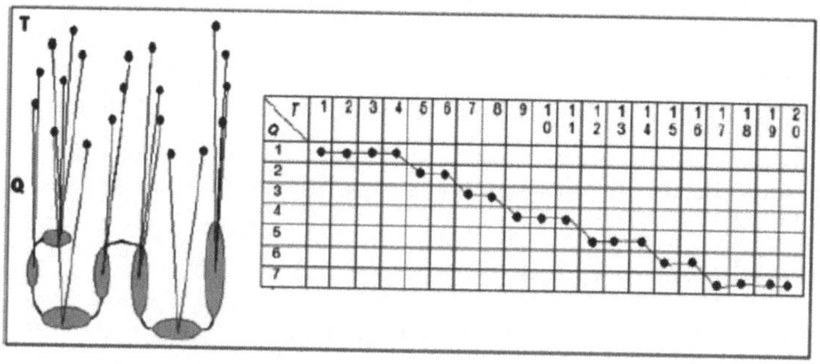


**Fig. 23.1. Transitions between states in SDTW**

SDTW distance is the negative log state optimized likelihood of pattern T generated by the model Q, with optimal state sequence S, given by the Viterbi algorithm. So, models in SDTW frame work are similar to HMMs of particular type with state prior probabilities .=(100…0)T and are left to right models with step size of at most 1 and with null transitions (transitions that allow change in state without observation change i.e. transitions (0,1) ). So the models in SDTW frame work can be trained by algorithms used for training HMMs. In our work, we used segmental K-means algorithm[3] for training SDTW model parameters.

*Unicode Generation*: Based on rules derived from the language, valid Unicode string is generated from the output labels of the classifier. This string is the input for the TTS module.

## Details of the TTS Module

The TTS is based on concatenative waveform synthesis[4]. There are 1026 phonetically rich sentences spoken by a professional Tamil speaker, which has been segmented and annotated at the phone level. The input text is passed through a grapheme to phoneme conversion module, after text normalization. Certain pause rules are added based on a preliminary PoS tagger and several rules. The phonemic text is parsed into the basic units for concatenation and the units are searched for, from the synthesis speech database, based on context and prosodic parameters. The selected speech units are concatenated in the waveform domain using a pitch continuity metric[5] and a pitch synchronous concatenation methodology[6]. It takes directly Unicode Tamil text as the input and produces a .wav file as the output. This wav file is directly played by the tablet PC and hence, when the user writes a word, it will be read after a second by the system.

## REFERENCES


1. Clauss Bahlmann and Hans Burkhardt , "The Writer Independent Online Handwriting Recognition System Frog On Hand and Cluster Generative Statistical Dynamic Time Warping", *IEEE Transactions on Pattern Analysis and Machine Intelligence*, Vol. 26, No. 3, pp. 299-310, March 2004.
2. Rituraj Kunwar *et al*. A HMM-based Online Tamil Word Recognizer, 8thTamil Internet Conference, 2009,University of Cologne , Germany.
3. Rakesh Dugad and U. B. Desai "*A Tutorial on Hidden Markov Models*",SPANN- 96.1 May 1996.
4. K Parthasarathy, "A Research Bed for Unit Selection Based Text to Speech Synthesis System", MS Thesis, Department of Electrical Engineering, IISc Bangalore, February 2009.
5. Vikram Ramesh Lakkavalli, Arulmozhi P and A G Ramakrishnan, "Continuity Metric for Unit Selection-based Text-to-Speech Synthesis", Accepted for Oral Presentation at SPCOM 2010, Bangalore, July 23-26.
6. Vikram Ramesh Lakkavalli and Ramakrishnan AG, "A Novel Method of Epoch Extraction for Concatenative Text-to-Speech Speech Synthesis" submitted to Interspeech 2010, Japan, September 26-30, 2010.

24

# Realization of Tamil Syllables Text to Speech Transferring System Using FPGA

— *T. Jayasankar, Dr. J. Arputha Vijaya Selvi and Prof. R. Rajendran*

***ABSTRACT***

*Design and development of the functional architecture of Tamil TTS engine using Field Programmable Gate Array (FPGA) is reported. It is a stand alone hardware system without any operating system (OS) to sense, identify and convert the Tamil mono-syllable text to speech output which is important for the visually impaired persons. The proposed model in FPGAs optimises the parameter extraction to perform efficient speech synthesis.*

***Keywords***— *Tamil text to speech, FPGA.*

## Introduction

Text to Speech (TTS) Synthesis is an automated encoding process which converts a sequence of symbols (text) conveying linguistic information, in to an acoustic waveform (speech).In recent years, text to speech synthesis technologies for different language are growing rapidly. Speech synthesis based on syllables seems to be a good possibility to enhance the quality of synthesized speech. As far as the production of speech is concerned, syllable is the minimum possible speech segment which can be spoken in isolation.

A Tamil voice system is expected to pave way for developing creative applications to enable users to hear Tamil content in voice form. The key concept behind this voice engine is Text-To-Speech conversion. This conversion uses the method of concatenating the syllables to generate the required words. A system used for this purpose is called a speech synthesizer and can be implemented in software or hardware. Hardware implementation of the above system is achieved by FPGA [Cyclone–II], and Verilog HDL and synthesizer tools. Minimal hardware makes the system to achieve cost effective, compact, very less power consumption and speed.

## Introduction to Tamil Languages

Over 65 million people worldwide speak Tamil, the official language of the southern state of Tamil Nadu, and also of Singapore, Sri Lanka and Mauritius. It will be a boom to Tamilian, if the user interface with the system is in Tamil, that too if it is in the form of speech.

## Nature of Tamil Scripts

The basic units of the writing system in Indian languages are characters which are an orthographic representation of speech sounds. A character in Indian language scripts is close to a syllable and can be typically of the form: $C^*VC^*$, where C is a consonant and V is a vowel. There is fairly good correspondence between what is written and what is spoken. Typically there are about 35 consonant and 18 vowel characters. However, in Tamil there are fewer characters than many of the other Indian languages. There are 13 vowels and 18 consonants characters. Some of the consonants have more than one pronunciation and in effect there are 41 phones.

## Creation of Tamil Speech Database

To build a unit selection voice, typically a small set of letter is recorded by a native Tamil speaker in a recording studio. The speaker uttered the sentences into a stand mounted microphone placed in front of her or his. The speech data was recorded at 44 KHz, mono channel at 16 bits per sample. After the recording it was down sampled to 16 KHz for further processing.

## Experimental Setup

The module used the previously stored phonetics sound to reproduce the word. The actual process of this project is by pressing a key in the PS/2 keyboard which is connected to the ALTERA DE1 board, a particular Tamil syllable which is pre-recorded in the SD card should be play backed.

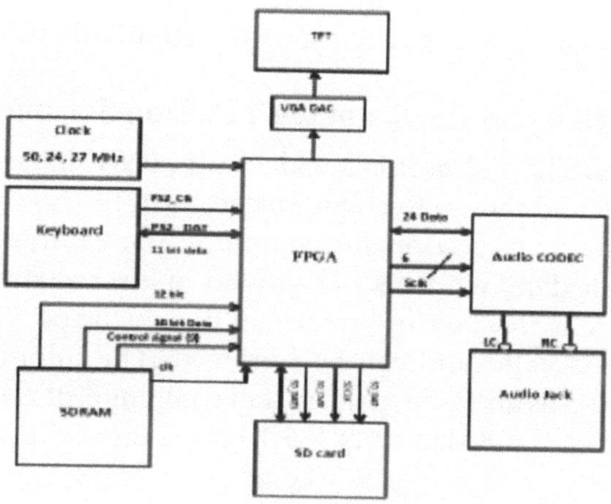


**Fig. 24.1: Data Flow in TS System**

Here 2 tools are used,

1. Quartus II tool and,
2. NIOS II IDE.

In the Quartus II tool, by using SOPC builder, the hardware components and their connections are created. By using NIOS, the software coding is developed. SD CARD acts as the pre-recorded component (recoded format of Tamil syllables).

SD card is inserted into the SD card driver of the DE1 board and the protocol used here is SP1 mode. When the program is started, the contents of SD card are moved to the FPGA and from there it is sent to audio codec through I2C protocol bus. On the audio codec the Tamil syllables gets processed and play backed.

Input to the system is the scan code of the keyboard which is connected through PS/2 connector of the DE1. By pressing a key, for e.g., by pressing V the scan code of 2A gets compared with the corresponding recorded Tamil syllables. For V the syllable of 'va' will be heard and gets displayed. If the incoming scan code has no recorded syllable means, it will play back the default values. (*i.e.,*) the scan code gets compared and the particular memory content is played.

## Description and Design of the TTS Transferring System

***Keyboard*:** The PS2 port is a widely supported interface for a keyboard and mouse to communicate with the host. The PS2 port contains two wires for communication purposes. One wire is for data, which is transmitted in a serial stream. The other wire is for the clock information, which specifies when the data is valid and can be retrieved. The information is transmitted as an 11-bit 'packet' that contains a start bit (Logic 0) followed by 8 data bits (LSB First), one odd parity bit (odd parity), and a stop bit (Logic

(1) Each bit should be read on the falling edge of the clock.

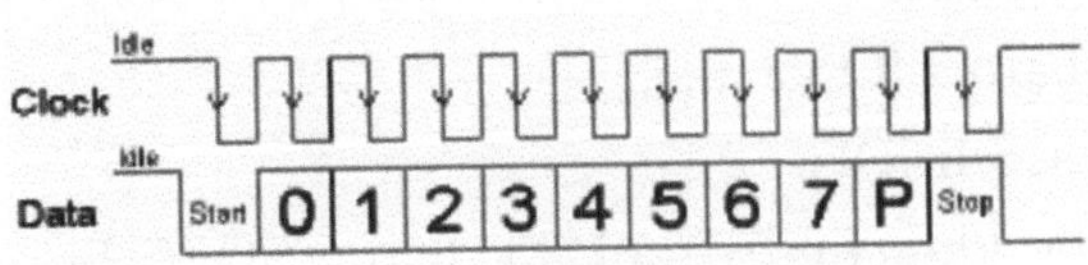


**Fig. 24.2: Timing diagram of a PS2 port**

The above waveform represents a one byte transmission from the Keyboard. The keyboard may not generally change its data line on the rising edge of the clock as shown in the diagram. The data line only has to be valid on the falling edge of the clock. The Keyboard will generate the clock. The frequency of the clock signal typically ranges from 20 to 30 KHz. The Least Significant Bit is always sent first.

The system hardware architecture is shown in figure 24.3 including CPU, UART, tri-state Bridge, ram and I/O controls, which are all reusable. Such design methods not only makes it Modulization, but also greatly reduce the design cycle of the system.

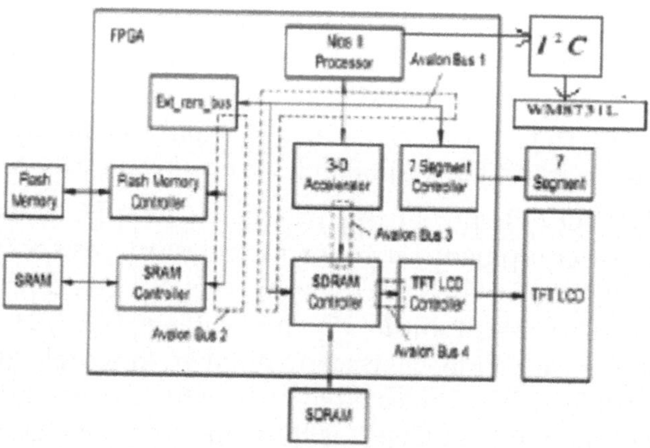


**Fig. 24.3: Hardware architecture**

***NIOS II Softcore Processor*:** Nios II is a high performance 32-bit softcore processor. The processor is configured on an Altera Cyclone II FPGA. Custom instructions are added to improve system performance; furthermore, more on-chip rams can be added to improve data processing capacity. SD card: Many applications use a large external storage device, such as a SD card or CF card, to store data. The DE1 board provides the hardware and software needed for SD card access. The size of the SD card should be less or equal to 2GB. Also, it is required to be formatted as FAT (FAT16 or FAT 32) File

System in advance. The system requires a 50 MHz clock provided from the board. The SD 1-bit protocol and FAT File System function are all implemented by NIOS II software. The software is stored in the onboard SDRAM memory.

***SDRAM***: In order to store the reference, the 512 kB SRAM module built in the board is used. There are three memory modules on the Altera DE2: a 4 MB Flash memory chip, an 8 MB SDRAM chip and a 512 kB SRAM chip. While the Flash module provides a vast amount of non-volatile storage, it is very slow with respect to the main system clock. The SDRAM chip is very fast and has a very large storage capacity, but it require a very sophisticated controller to be operated. This makes the SRAM chip an obvious choice. Even though it is not the fastest nor the largest, it has ten times the required storage capacity needed for this project, and it is fast enough (since it can perform a read or write operation in less than 20 ns, i.e. a system clock period) so as to avoid any timing issues. Moreover, it is a fairly simple device and can easily control.

***AUDIO CODEC***: In this project the CODEC is used as both test equipment for other modules and as secondary input/output for the audio system. The DE1 board provides high-quality 24-bit audio via the Wolfson WM8731 audio CODEC. The WM8731 is controlled by a serial I2C bus interface, which is connected to pins on the Cyclone II FPGA. Initialization of the CODEC is through a standard I2C (Inter-Integrated Circuit) bus and sound transfer is through a 3-wire bus, which in this project is defined as a standard I2S (Inter-IC Sound) bus.

Figure 24.4 above shows the structure of the CODEC connection to the control numbers on the CODEC are generated using the NIOS II processor. This chip supports microphone-in, line-in, and line-out ports, with a sample rate adjustable from 8 kHz to 96 kHz. WM8731 contains A/D, D/A modules with a high sample rate and quantization precision. We will use 8kHz sample rate and 16 bit quantization precision in this design.

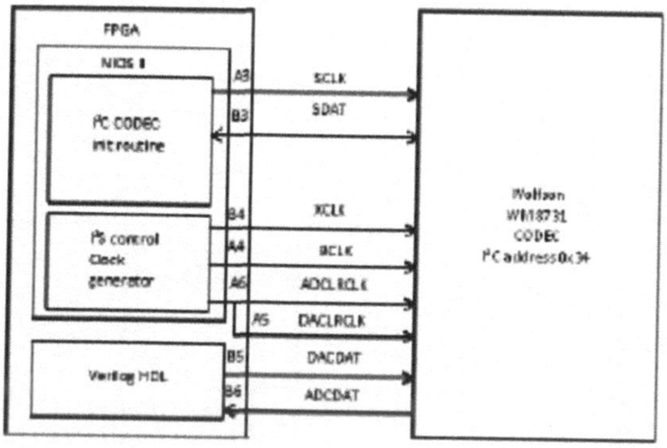


**Fig. 24.4: Connection diagram of CODEC part of the DEI board**

In voice acquisition part, since A/D is the serial data output, a serial to parallel data conversion and control of the SRAM Verilog module is needed. Voice report is communicated with CPU via GPIO; different voice is played according to different verification result. GPIO control is done in Nios IDE. Similarly, since the voice broadcast from FLASH are read out in parallel, thus a parallel to serial data conversion Verilog module is needed.

**TFT LCD display**: The 3.6" LCD module is the active matrix colour TFT LCD module. LTPS (Low Temperature Poly Silicon) TFT technology is used and vertical and horizontal drivers are built on the panel. Horizontal scan can be from left to right or from right to left and vertical scan can be from up to down or from Down to up. We developed the LCD Controller and displayed a Tamil text to the TFT LCD. The main CPU is the Nios II processor.

The Nios II processor connects to ext_RAM_bus, 3-D accelerator, 7-segment controller, SDRAM controller, TFT-LCD controller, and so on. The ext_RAM_bus module is a tristate Avalon bus bridge that connects the Nios II processor to flash memory and SRAM, which are the instruction memory and data memory, respectively, used to run the Nios II processor.

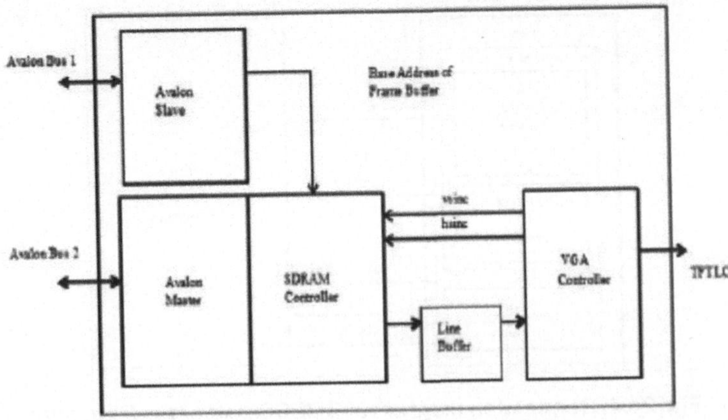


**Fig. 24.5: STFT interfacing module**

New Component menu option in SOPC Builder is used to include the LCD Controller module and specify its signals. The signals between the LCD Controller and Avalon bus became the pins of the Nios II module. The slave side of the module is connected to the Nios II processor and the master side is connected to the SDRAM controller.

## Proposed Design Flow Algorithm

- Initialize and load the acoustic library, which consists all the audio recordings;
- Load the target or input word; initialize the register counter;
- While (target letter match to memory address) do
- Wave files play via audio codec from the corresponding memory address;
- when player done = 1 implies audio player has finished playing the wave file;
- /* end the loop*/
- reset the register counter ;
- repeat the procedure for all the target letter;

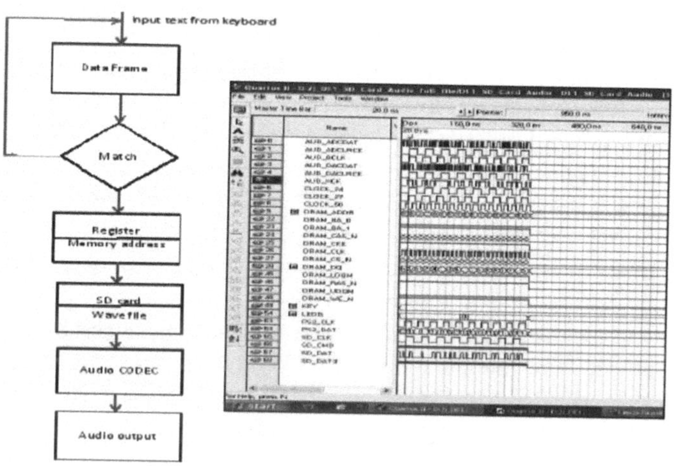


The project is simulated using Verilog in Altera tools. Simulation for the sound of 'a'(in Tamil).

**Fig. 24.6: Design Flow of the TTS Simulation Results**

The project is simulated using Verilog in Altera tools. Simulation for the sound of 'a'(in Tamil).

## Conclusion

In this chapter, the design and development of functional architecture of Tamil text to speech synthesis is described. Different feature streams are experimented with the system that optimises the parameter extraction to perform efficient speech synthesis.

## Future Work

This work can be extended for concatenating the Tamil syllables and also produce the natural Tamil voice from FPGA based machine.

## REFERENCES

1. R.Thangarajan, "*Syllable-based Continuous Speech Recognition for Tamil*", in South Asian language review, 2008.

2. Nageshwararao and Hema, "*Text to Speech Synthesis Using Syllable Like Unit*", 2005 IEEE Paper.
3. P. Nirmala Devi and R. Asokan "VLSI Implementation of Speech to Text Conversion" in *Proceedings of International Conference of Intelligent Knowledge Systems* (IKS-2004), Turkey, 2004.
4. G.L. Jayawardhana Rama and A.G Ramakrishna "A Complete Text to Speech Synthesis' System in Tamil" *IEEE Workshop on Speech Synthesis*, 2002.
5. B.H.Juang," Why Speech Synthesis?" *IEEE Transactions on Speech and Audio Processing*, 2001
6. A.G.Ramakrishnan, "Thirukural Text to Speech Synthesis System", proco. Tamil Internet 2001, Kuala Lumpur
7. Pong P.Chu, "FPGA Prototyping by Verilog Examples", John Wiley &Sons, 2008
8. Douglas O'Shaughnessy, "*Speech Communication*", Universities Press, 2004, Second Edition.
9. http://www.altera.com/literature/manual/mnl_cii_starter_board_rm.pdf

25

# A High Accuracy Phone Recognition System for Tamil

— C. P. Santosh Kumar and N. Deiva Sundaram

**ABSTRACT**

*Phone recognition systems are used in many applications such as automatic segmentation of speech, keyword spotting, automatic language identification using phonotactic approach, and speaker identification. Phone recognition accuracy and the accuracy of the application developed are highly correlated. In this chapter, we present the details of a high accuracy phone recognition system developed for Tamil. We use a hybrid hidden Markov model—neural network to implement the decoder. It was seen that for moderate data sizes, the system outperforms the hidden Markov model—Gaussian mixture model implementations.*

## Introduction

High accuracy phone recognition systems are very useful for many applications. They can be helpful for phonetic labelling of speech; speech data collected with the word level transcriptions without any segmentation information can be converted to phonetic transcriptions with segmentation information. If this segmentation information has to be generated manually, we will need an experienced phonetician, and doing this manually is not cost effective. Further, due to the co-articulation effects, the segmentation boundaries thus obtained will not be precise. Under such conditions, a consistent phone boundary is the best choice, and a machine assisted segmentation and labelling using a phone recognizer can be more effective and cost effective. Phone recognition systems are also used in automatic keyword spotting systems using phone lattices, language identification using phonotactic approach, and speaker identification. Performance of these systems is highly correlated with the phone recognition accuracy and therefore any effort to enhance the phone recognition accuracy is likely to enhance the performance of the application.

Hidden Markov model—Gaussian mixture model (HMM-GMM) are known for their performance in the development of speech recognition systems, and in such systems Gaussian mixture models are used to model the probability distributions. In speech recognition systems, word n-gram language models and phone n-gram language models can be used to enhance the recognition accuracy. However, for moderate size databases hidden Markov model - neural network structures[1,2,3,4] have been found to offer better performance compared to the HMM-GMM systems, and for large databases both offer similar performances, but HMM-NN systems has less complexity.

Segments of speech (frames) represented in terms of their probabilistic similarity to the phones of any language are often referred as probabilistic features (PF)[1, 2]. Temporal patterns (TRAPS)[1] of log energy from critical bands is a way to derive PFs. In[1, 2], several band-conditioned classifiers are used to derive PF to be merged by a neural network to estimate the phone posteriors. The use of band conditioned phone posteriors as temporal features was studied in[3]. In this work, they used the hidden layer activation outputs, and is known as hidden activation TRAPS (HATS). In[4], a simplified system offering better results, and requiring less training data due to the splitting of TRAPS features to left and right context has become popular since[4] due to its simplicity and ability to reduce the amount of training data required for similar performances. In this work, we use the implementation in[4] to implement a high accuracy phone recognizer for Tamil.

Keyword spotting systems (KWS)[5,6] are useful for archiving and indexing audio/video documents to be searched using keywords, searching for telephonic conversations that contain words/phrases that are potentially dangerous to the national security, and thereby derive intelligence information. Large vocabulary continuous speech recognition (LVCSR) system based KWS are very popular for their better performance. However, they have many limitations to be applied directly to the Indian environment. To develop an LVCSR system for a language, we need a large labelled speech database to train the acoustic models, and to the best of our knowledge, such a database is not yet available for Tamil. In the Indian context, we tend to use words/phrases across languages, and is fairly common to mix words/phrases from English in native language conversations. LVCSR systems cannot handle multiple languages at the same time, as it needs a language model to enhance the word recognition accuracy, and training a language model catering for multiple languages is practically impossible for many reasons. In this work, we present the details of a KWS systems developed using the lattices[5] generated by the HMM-NN phone recognizer. Another approach that is widely popular uses lattices generated by a phone recognizer[5, 6]. This approach has the advantage that it can be easily ported to multilingual environments, unlike the LVCSR based approach[5] gives a comparison of different KWS approaches.

## HMM-NN Phone Recognizer

In the hybrid HMM-NN system, critical band energies are obtained in the conventional way[1, 2, 3, 4], Speech signal is divided into 25 ms long frames with 10 ms shift. The Mel filter-bank is emulated by triangular weighting of FFT-derived short-term spectrum to obtain short-term critical-band logarithmic spectral densities. TRAPS feature vector describes a segment of temporal evolution of critical band spectral densities within a single critical band. The central point is the current frame and 15 frames from the past make a left context (LC) feature and similarly 15 frames from the future make the right context (RC) feature vector. Further, the LC and RC features are windowed to make the transition between the successive frames smooth. Triangular window was used for this purpose. Subsequently, these feature vectors are processed for dimensionality reduction. We used Discrete Cosine Transform (DCT) for its simplicity to reduce the 16 dimensional LC and RC feature sizes to 11[1, 2, 3, 4]. To further enhance the accuracy of the system, we concatenated 15 critical band features for LC and RC to generate input to two separate LC and RC neural networks. Outputs of these classifiers are subsequently merged together using another neural net. Outputs of all neural networks represent phone state posterior probabilities, and phone models have three states each. Details of the implementation can be found in[3, 4], Fig. 25.1 illustrates the schematic diagram of the implementation of the LC-RC HMM-NN phone recognizer.

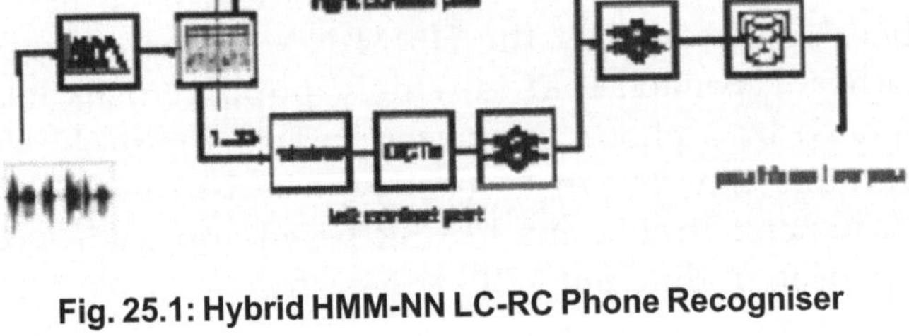

**Fig. 25.1: Hybrid HMM-NN LC-RC Phone Recogniser**

Table 25.1.

| Phone (ASCII) | Alphabet – Example Transcription | Phone (ASCII) | Alphabet – Example Transcription |
|---|---|---|---|
| ax | அ - அம்மா /ax m m aa/ | ay | எ - எட்டு /ae t t U/ |
| aa | ஆ - ஆடு /aa d U/ | ey | ஏ - ஏணி /ey nn ih/ |
| ih | இ - இலை / ih l ax y/ | ao | ஒ - ஒன்று /ao n dr U/ |
| iy | ஈ - ஈசல் /iy [illegible] ax y/ | ow | ஓ - ஓம் /ow m/ |
| uh | உ - உணவு /uh nn ax v U/ | aw | ஔ - ஔவை /aw v ax y/ |
| U | உ - தப்பு /th ax p p U/ | | |
| uw | ஊ - ஊர் /uw r/ | | |

Table 25.2.

| Phone (ASCII) | Alphabet – Example Transcription | Phone (ASCII) | Alphabet – Example Transcription |
|---|---|---|---|
| k | க் - கல்வி /k ax l v ih/ | dh | ந் - பந்தம் /p ax nd dh ax m/ |
| g | க் - பங்கு /p ax ng g U/ | nd | ந் - பந்து /p ax nd dh U/ |
| ng | ங் - தங்கம் /th ax ng g ax m/ | p | ப் - பாடம் /p aa d ax m/ |
| ch | ச் - காட்சி /k aa t ch ih/ | b | ப் - அம்பு /ax m b U/ |
| jh | ஜ - ஜாதி /j aa th ih/ | P | ப் - ஸோபா /s ao P aa/ |
| ny | ஞ் - ஞானம் /ny aa n ax m/ | m | ம் - கரும்பு /k ax r uh m b U/ |
| t | ட் - அட்டை /ax t t ey/ | y | ய் - யமுனை /y ax m uh n ax y/ |
| d | ட் - கடல் /k ax d ax l/ | r | ர் - மரம் /m ax r ax m/ |
| nn | மணி /m ax nn ih/ | tr | ற் - ஒற்றன் /ao t tr ax n/ |
| ddn | ண் - கண் /k ax ddn/ | dr | ற் - கன்று /k ax n dr U/ |
| th | த் - தட்டு /th ax t t U/ | rr | ற் - அறம் /ax rr ax m/ |
| Th | த் - மதி /m ax Th ih/ | l | ல் - மாலை /m aa l ax y/ |
| h | பட்டம் /p ah t t ah m/ | ll | ள் - உள்ளம் /uh ll ll ax m/ |
| sh | ஷ் - விஷம் /v ih sh ax m/ | lzh | ழ் - பழம் /p ax lzh ax m/ |
| s | ச் - அஞ்சு /ax nj s U/ | v | வ் - வயது /v ax y ax dh U/ |
| hh | க் - பக்ஸ் /p ax hh ax l/ | n | ன் - நான் /n aa n/ |

## Lattice-based KWS System

Lattices[7] are a way of storing output of a recognizer as an oriented acyclic graph in which each node represent a symbol (phone) and each link represent time boundaries of the phone/ word at the end of the link. Fig. 25.2 shows an example lattice generated by a phone recognizer. It may be seen that at any instant in time, there are multiple possibilities available when the keywords are to be searched. Searching in lattices provides better results than searching in phone strings[5] as it holds several hypotheses in parallel. We follow a lattice based approach in this work[5, 6]. Phone lattices were generated from phone posteriori probabilities. In our experiments phone insertion penalty was set to zero for lattice generation to minimize deletion of phones. Fig. 25.2 shows the schematic representation of the KWS system implemented in this paper, and the likelihood of the keywords are compared with the likelihoods of the hypothesis generated by the background filler phone models working in a parallel loop to decide the presence or absence of a keyword in a continuously spoken sentence.

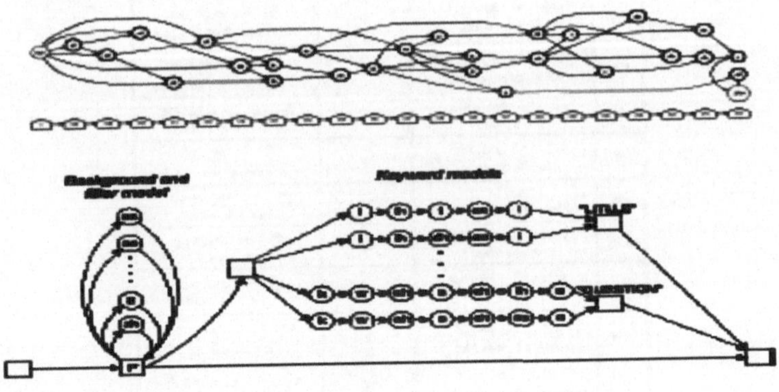

Fig. 25.2.

## Experiments and Results

We used 1.2 hours of telephone quality speech sampled at 8

kHz for our experiments. In the HMM-NN systems, we used 300 neurons for modeling the probability distribution. For the HMM-GMM systems, we used 16 Gaussians to model the probability distributions, and the models are trained using maximum mutual information criteria using the HTK toolkit[7]. The size of the neural network and the GMMs was chosen to match the limited training data available.

**Table 25.3.**

| HMM-GMM | HMM-NN |
|---|---|
| 51.87 | 56.62 |

KWS systems are evaluated using Figure-of-Merit (FOM)[6], which is the average of correct detections per 1, 2, . . . 10 false alarms per hour. We used the most frequently occurring 60 words to benchmark our system. The KWS system developed in this using the HMM-NN phone recognizer gave an FOM of 66.25 per cent for the most frequently used 60 words in the test set.

## REFERENCES

1. H. Hermansky, and S. Sharma, TRAPS—Classifiers of Temporal Patterns, Proc. ICSLP, Sydney, Nov. 1998
2. H. Hermansky, D.P.W. Ellis, and S. Sharma, Tandem Connectionist Feature Extraction for Conventional HMM Systems, Proc. ICASSP 2000, Turkey, 2000.
3. B. Chen, Q. Zhu, and N.Morgan, Learning Long-term Temporal Features in LVCSR Using Neural Networks, Proc. ICSLP, Jeju Island, October 2004.
4. P. Schwarz, P. Matejka, and J. Cernocky: Towards Lower Error Rates in Phoneme Recognition, in Proc. TSD 2004, Brno, Czech Republic, 2004
5. I. Szoke and P Schwarz and P. Matejka and L. Burget and M. Karafi'at and M. Fapso and J. Cernock'y, Comparison of Keyword Spotting Approaches for Informal Continuous Speech, Interspeech 2005—Eurospeech, Lisaboa, Portugal, September 2005, pp. 633–636.

6. M. Saraclar and R. Sproat, Lattice-based Search for Spoken Utterance Retrieval, Human Language Technology Conference of the North American Chapter of the Association for Computational Inguistics (hlt-naacl2004), Boston, Massachusetts, USA, May, 2004.
7. CUED, HTK Toolkit, http://htk.eng.cam.ac.uk/

# Index

**Q**



**R**

**T**